Business Guides on the Go

"Business Guides on the Go" presents cutting-edge insights from practice on particular topics within the fields of business, management, and finance. Written by practitioners and experts in a concise and accessible form the series provides professionals with a general understanding and a first practical approach to latest developments in business strategy, leadership, operations, HR management, innovation and technology management, marketing or digitalization. Students of business administration or management will also benefit from these practical guides for their future occupation/careers.

These Guides suit the needs of today's fast reader.

Sandra Gauer

Leadership in New Working Environments

Realizing the Potential of Flexible Workplace Concepts

Sandra Gauer
Gauer Consulting
Bern, Switzerland

ISSN 2731-4758 ISSN 2731-4766 (electronic)
Business Guides on the Go
ISBN 978-3-031-50433-4 ISBN 978-3-031-50434-1 (eBook)
https://doi.org/10.1007/978-3-031-50434-1

© The Editor(s) (if applicable) and The Author(s), under exclusive license to Springer Nature Switzerland AG 2024
This work is subject to copyright. All rights are solely and exclusively licensed by the Publisher, whether the whole or part of the material is concerned, specifically the rights of reprinting, reuse of illustrations, recitation, broadcasting, reproduction on microfilms or in any other physical way, and transmission or information storage and retrieval, electronic adaptation, computer software, or by similar or dissimilar methodology now known or hereafter developed.
The use of general descriptive names, registered names, trademarks, service marks, etc. in this publication does not imply, even in the absence of a specific statement, that such names are exempt from the relevant protective laws and regulations and therefore free for general use.
The publisher, the authors, and the editors are safe to assume that the advice and information in this book are believed to be true and accurate at the date of publication. Neither the publisher nor the authors or the editors give a warranty, expressed or implied, with respect to the material contained herein or for any errors or omissions that may have been made. The publisher remains neutral with regard to jurisdictional claims in published maps and institutional affiliations.

This Springer imprint is published by the registered company Springer Nature Switzerland AG
The registered company address is: Gewerbestrasse 11, 6330 Cham, Switzerland

Paper in this product is recyclable

Contents

1 **Leadership and New Worlds of Work** 1
 1.1 A Multi-Layered Subject and Minefield 1
 1.2 Transformational Leadership in New Work Settings 2

2 **New Work Environments: A Strategic Process** 13
 2.1 In the Beginning Was the Thought 13
 2.2 Recognising and Disentangling Complexity 14
 2.3 Consider Different Levels 15
 2.4 The Iceberg Model by Gauer 16
 2.5 What Does this Mean for Leadership? 23
  2.5.1 For Managers 23
  2.5.2 For Employees 24
 2.6 Building New Working Environments in a Meaningful Way 24
  2.6.1 Recognising Potentials 25
  2.6.2 Actively Involving Employees 25
  2.6.3 Enabling Leadership 25
  2.6.4 Designing the Office According to Needs 25

	2.7	Human Resources and the New World of Work	26
	2.7.1	Corporate Values as a Driving Force	26
	2.7.2	Interaction Between Manager and Human Resources Department	27

3 New Working Environments Create Stress — 29
- 3.1 Positive and Negative Stress — 29
- 3.2 Acting in an Evolutionary-Biological Yet Socially Correct Way — 30
- 3.3 The Office as a Risk Area: A Development — 32
- 3.4 The Stressors Right in Front of you — 33
- 3.5 We Overtake Ourselves — 34
- 3.6 Resilience Also Means Being Realistic — 36
- 3.7 Dealing with Stressors: The Theory — 37
- 3.8 Actively Confronting the Stress Issue — 38
- 3.9 Dealing with Stressors: An Approach — 38
- 3.10 What Does this Mean for Leadership? — 42

4 Discover Efficiency Killers — 45
- 4.1 Constant Interruptions — 45
- 4.2 Technostress — 46
  - 4.2.1 Simultaneity and Diversity Are a Serious Problem — 47
  - 4.2.2 Technostress as a Clinical Picture — 47
  - 4.2.3 Surprising Research — 47
- 4.3 Smartphones Waste our Brain Power — 48
  - 4.3.1 Three Groups Examined — 48
  - 4.3.2 Surprising Result — 49
  - 4.3.3 Brain Power Is Wasted — 49
- 4.4 What Does this Mean for Leadership? — 49
  - 4.4.1 For Managers — 49
  - 4.4.2 For Employees — 50

5 Conflicts in New Working Environments — 53
- 5.1 It Is Not Immediately a Conflict — 53
- 5.2 Types of Conflict — 54

5.3	Conflict Phenomena		54
5.4	There Is Potential for Conflict Everywhere		56
5.5	What Does this Mean for Leadership?		58
	5.5.1	For Managers	58
	5.5.2	For Employees	59

6 The Human in the Field of Tension Between the Real and the Virtual World — 61
- 6.1 Cool Environments, Styled Layouts, Happy Office — 61
- 6.2 Work Routes Must Be Used Efficiently — 62
  - 6.2.1 Collaboration Is Changing — 62
  - 6.2.2 Why the Office Is Also Changing — 64
  - 6.2.3 Architecture and the Impact on Occupational Psychology — 64
  - 6.2.4 The Office Performance Model — 65

7 The Power of the Built Environment on our Experience and Behaviour — 67
- 7.1 Architectural-Psychological Perspectives — 67
- 7.2 Recognising Connections — 69
- 7.3 Maslow's Experiment — 70
- 7.4 We Can Contribute — 70
- 7.5 Art Nouveau and New Working Worlds — 71

8 The Virtual Space — 73
- 8.1 Out of the Office or in the Office? — 73
- 8.2 Work Life and Private Life Blur Together — 75
- 8.3 Team Spirit Decreases but Employer Attractiveness Increases — 76
- 8.4 Loneliness — 77
- 8.5 Trust Among Colleagues — 78
- 8.6 Trust in Superiors — 81
- 8.7 What Does this Mean for Leadership? — 83
  - 8.7.1 For Managers — 83
  - 8.7.2 For Employees — 84

9 The Physical Space — 87
- 9.1 Leadership and Architecture — 87
- 9.2 Architectural and Psychological Success Factors — 88
  - 9.2.1 Designing Spaces: Work-Related and Architectural Factors — 89
  - 9.2.2 Understanding People: Structural and Psychological Factors — 90
  - 9.2.3 People and Architecture: An Interplay — 90
- 9.3 Research Findings — 92
  - 9.3.1 Employees Enjoy Working in the Office — 92
  - 9.3.2 Managers Prefer Going to the Office to Employees — 93
  - 9.3.3 Private Areas Are Also Very Important in the Office — 94
- 9.4 What Does this Mean for Leadership? — 96
  - 9.4.1 For Managers — 96
  - 9.4.2 For Employees — 97

10 Emotional Leadership as a Booster for New Work Environments — 99
- 10.1 What Employees Want — 100
- 10.2 How Much Can a Leader Give? — 100
  - 10.2.1 Too Few Workers for Future Economic Performance — 101
  - 10.2.2 Problem Factor Quiet Quitting — 102
- 10.3 How Much Responsibility Does a Manager Have to Take on? — 102
- 10.4 New Working Environments: An Emotional Process — 103
  - 10.4.1 Transformation Is a Challenge — 103
  - 10.4.2 Leadership Is the Balance Between Desires and Possibilities — 104

Further Reading — 107

List of Figures

Fig. 1.1   The concept of transformational leadership. The concept explains how leaders need to act to inspire loyalty, eagerness to learn new things, team spirit, self-discipline, responsibility and improved performance in their employees (Institute for Management Innovation (Pelz))   4

Fig. 1.2   Model of transformational leadership in new work environments. The model shows which competences and behaviours employees need to develop in order to work efficiently in new work environments and how managers need to act to foster them (Gauer Consulting)   7

Fig. 1.3   Core features of leadership in new working environments (Gauer Consulting)   8

Fig. 2.1   Vision, strategy and leadership. New work environments—from the vision to the product and the dual role of leadership (Gauer Consulting)   14

Fig. 2.2   Integration of psychological, architectural and psychological aspects in the design of new working environments to promote performance, satisfaction and health (Gauer Consulting)   15

Fig. 2.3   The Iceberg Model. The model shows the multi-layered nature and complexity of new working environments through differently visible levels, which need to be taken into account in initiatives to introduce new working environments (Gauer Consulting)   16

List of Figures

Fig. 2.4	The visible layer of working environments (Gauer Consulting)	18
Fig. 2.5	The partially visible layer of working environments (Gauer Consulting)	19
Fig. 2.6	The invisible layer of working environments (Gauer Consulting)	21
Fig. 2.7	Designing the office according to needs (Gauer Consulting)	26
Fig. 3.1	The stress curve. A certain level of stress can promote motivation and performance (Gauer Consulting)	30
Fig. 3.2	Possible physical and psychological consequences of negative stress (Gauer Consulting)	31
Fig. 3.3	Framework programme of holistic health in companies. A practice-oriented framework programme by Gauer Consulting that combines stress theory and pandemic-related aspects with organisational influences and consequences (Gauer Consulting)	39
Fig. 3.4	Concrete action steps for companies based on the framework programme of holistic health in companies (Fig. 3.3) (Gauer Consulting)	40
Fig. 5.1	Different types of conflict (Gauer Consulting)	55
Fig. 5.2	Conflict management model. Conflict potential in new working environments and workplace change initiatives (Gauer Consulting)	57
Fig. 6.1	Expectations of companies regarding their future workplace based on the mentioned findings from Steelcase (Gauer Consulting)	63
Fig. 6.2	The Office Performance Model (OPM). This model is the foundation for the strategic orientation, planning, implementation and utilisation of workplace change projects (Gauer Consulting)	66
Fig. 7.1	Simplified schematic representation of the cross-hierarchical village structure of the Bororo tribe in South America (left figure) and the structure introduced by missionaries according to the European row house principle (right figure) (Gauer Consulting)	68
Fig. 7.2	Mental and physical well-being in physical space. Architectural and individual factors affect the perception of environmental conditions and influence psychological and physical well-being both through this mediator and directly (Gauer Consulting)	69

List of Figures

Fig. 9.1 The connection between people and architecture. It is important that the interplay between the experience and behaviour of people and architecture is taken into account in the design of new working environments (Gauer Consulting) 91

Fig. 9.2 Effects of employees enjoying working in the office on engagement, productivity, identification with the company culture and change of employer, based on Steelcase's findings mentioned in the text above (Gauer Consulting) 91

Fig. 9.3 Differences between employees and managers in terms of the availability of a private office in the company, the time they spend on focus work and whether they like working in the office, based on Steelcase's findings mentioned in the text (Gauer Consulting) 92

Fig. 9.4 What people value in the office based on Steelcase's findings mentioned in the text (Gauer Consulting) 95

List of Tables

Table 5.1	Further types of conflict and corresponding approaches to resolving them (adapted from Evangelischer Fachverband für Arbeit und soziale Integration (EFAS))	55
Table 5.2	Central conflict phenomena and their characterisation (adapted from Evangelischer Fachverband für Arbeit und soziale Integration (EFAS))	56

1

Leadership and New Worlds of Work

1.1 A Multi-Layered Subject and Minefield

How much do new working environments have to do with leadership?

Looking back on 17 years of consulting experience in this area, there is only one answer for me: everything!

Leaders at all levels of the hierarchy are the main characters in this exciting film about power, emotions, prestige, culture, performance and the question of meaning. New working environments are as cross-disciplinary and emotionally charged as hardly any other change process. This is probably also the reason why companies like to hide behind modern design and spatial concepts. Do not get me wrong, well-designed and thought-out interior layouts are important and right, but they are just the tip of the iceberg, the final cherry on top, the icing on the cake.

It is about us—reduced to the maximum. It is about us, about how we want to work, how we need to work, and what our part is. Managers in particular have a special role to play here, because they need to have a clear understanding of these questions themselves, and at the same time guide their employees into this new world.

1.2 Transformational Leadership in New Work Settings

I am often asked which leadership style is best suited for new working environments and new work. I believe that it is extremely important to find your own style and create your own mix. Ultimately, leadership is the sum of experience, attitude and personality.

The first question to ask is what new working environments are all about and what process they go through. The success of a workplace change initiative depends heavily on the commitment and understanding of its employees. What is unclear, however, is which leadership style is best suited to achieving this. In recent years, one leadership style has emerged that can do this. It is called transformational leadership.

This leadership style is called transformational because it can change employee behaviour. My experience has been, and still is, that people believe that change comes from handing out leadership guidelines, vision and mission statements and colourful brochures and holding workshops and paying a lot of money for nice interior design. And then everyone is surprised that change does happen, but usually in the form of more absenteeism, less productivity and more dissatisfaction. On top of that, companies are often not authentic in what they say and how they act.

I always talk about the role model function of leaders as the key to success. This is the be-all and end-all of leadership and *the* big success factor. The role model function has the greatest influence on the commitment and performance of employees and on how they use new working environments in an efficient and supportive way for themselves and the company.

And that brings me back to basic behaviour patterns. I like to illustrate this with an example: When I sit in a meeting with managers and we talk about leading by example in the introduction, support and use of new working environments, they usually confirm what I say and want to reassure me that they will definitely stand behind it and lead by example and commitment. When I look people in the eye, I notice that many of them don't really mean what they say. How can I tell? Psychologists talk about "honest signals"—gestures, facial expressions and behaviour. Researchers believe that the first spoken language emerged 500'000 years ago and has continued to develop ever since. Before that, we communicated with honest signals, which were unmistakable and unambiguous and had to be in order to survive. But now, although we have fully developed, even perfected, language, our non-verbal signals are still the same. And they give us away because they often contradict what we say.

If managers try to present something that they are not convinced about, do not know enough about, have not thought about, or simply cannot relate to—they will communicate this to their staff in a non-verbal way. Whether they want to or not. The role model function is a very sensitive issue, because it only works with the predicate "real".

So, the question is, what do managers need to do to make their employees want to learn new things, improve their performance, take responsibility, show self-discipline, act entrepreneurially and practice team spirit?

Part of the answer lies in the concept of transformational leadership (Fig. 1.1). But again, I see it as a guide and a generator of ideas. It only works with authenticity, knowledge and experience. We have to be careful that we do not apply the concept 1:1, but to adapt it in those elements that are suitable for the respective person.

So, let us have a look at the concept and see what the possibilities are.

Concept of Transformational Leadership[1]

The Institute for Management Innovation conducted around 300 interviews with mid-sized global market leaders and also surveyed around 30,000 specialists and managers online to find out what transformational leaders do differently from their colleagues.[2]

The results show what transformational leaders do differently from their peers. Let me give you a few examples to illustrate.

---

[1] Pelz, W. Transformationale Führung – Forschungsstand und Umsetzung in der Praxis. Wirksame und nachhaltige Führungsansätze: System, Beziehung, Haltung und Individualität. 2016:95.

[2] Pelz, W. Transformationale Führung: Vorteile und Wirkung (neue Studie). Available at: https://www.transformationale-fuehrung.com/index.html.

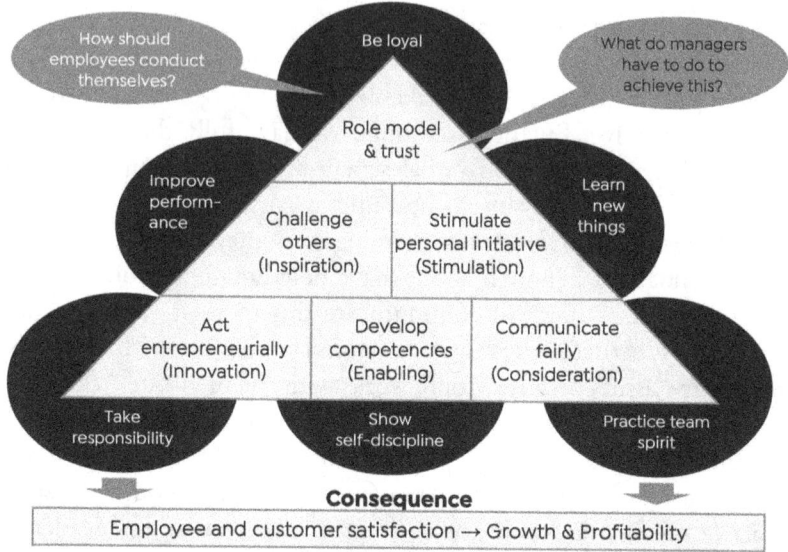

Fig. 1.1 The concept of transformational leadership. The concept explains how leaders need to act to inspire loyalty, eagerness to learn new things, team spirit, self-discipline, responsibility and improved performance in their employees (Institute for Management Innovation (Pelz))

1) They create trust because their personal goals, values and beliefs are authentic and credible. This enables them to implement the honest signals described above.
2) They put the common task before their personal interests, because leadership is about achieving goals with the team and implementing them successfully.
3) These leaders use their influence to translate the vision, with which everyone identifies, into measurable results.[3]

In this way, they create a sense of achievement, strengthen team spirit and promote personal growth. Their work has a clearly identifiable, long-term meaning for themselves and their employees.

---

[3] Pelz, W. Transformationale Führung: Vorteile und Wirkung (neue Studie). Available at: https://www.transformationale-fuehrung.com/index.html.

The renowned researcher Dr. Theo Wehner of ETH Zurich has clearly established the connection between the question of meaning and work performance.

Occupational psychology, I would say, has been satisfied with the study of general satisfaction. There is no book on occupational psychology that does not deal with this on many pages, there are many measuring instruments that have dealt with this. But this is only one side. Job satisfaction is more modest—and the conditions for high job satisfaction are also more modest than those defined in research on the sense of meaning.

And it is striking that there are relatively few entries under the keyword "meaning" in textbooks of work and organisational psychology, which then read "meaningfulness of the task". There it is seen as follows: the task must offer the possibility of generating meaning. And this clearly raises the question: does meaning attach itself to things? I think meaning is not something that is attached or tacked on, but meaning is something that is personally generated.

Can new working environments help to increase the sense of meaning?

We can create conditions in new work environments that are meaningful to individuals. As a leader, you have enormous leverage to use. But we must not forget that meaning is very personal. Holism, diversity of space requirements or workplace design in isolation do not guarantee a sense of meaning. And this is where the big stumbling blocks lie. It has to be a very difficult mix to create meaningful work environments.

The Austrian neurologist Viktor Frankl was one of the first to point out the importance of the meaning of the experience being processed. This means that workplaces provide experiences for people, and that people need to process these experiences in order to derive personal meaning from them. And it may well be that a work task is not holistic, or that you only do a small part of it, but you see that it is reasonable, useful, usable within the division of labour, and that you can then also generate meaning in the processing of this personal experience.

Terms such as "role model", "credibility", "trust" or "respect" are often used in theory and practice. Unfortunately, not only is it often unclear what is meant by them, but they are also spoken thoughtlessly. Managers want to be them, and employees want to have them. But too often it is forgotten that both sides have a responsibility regarding these things. It is like a marriage: You need to get closer to each other in order to be happy together, not just at the beginning when the rose-coloured glasses are blinding you. It is important to work together as a team to build on each other's strengths, support each other's weaknesses and sometimes to just accept. Leadership is a team effort, not an individual act. It is important that both sides recognise this to be truly sustainable role models, to live credibility, to have trust and to treat each other with respect.

Otherwise, they remain empty theatrical words that can be interpreted in all sorts of ways (the best example being "sustainability"). For this reason, the Institute for Management Innovation has operationalised these terms, in other words, made them measurable, and validated this concept (critically examined for practical relevance) in the context of transformational leadership with the sample of around 30'000 participants. The result is the Giessen Inventory of Transformational Leadership.[4] It follows a principle that is often attributed to Peter Drucker: "You can't manage what you don't measure". This also applies to new working environments, or rather, it is precisely there where it is about being successful in the short, medium and long term and using this new working environment in a meaningful way for oneself in order to work efficiently and at the same time to feel good and healthy and, above all, to stay that way.

The above-mentioned test is a tool that can be used to profile the strengths and weaknesses of transformational leadership competencies to derive targeted development measures. It is crucial to have an analysis phase to know where you stand and where you want to go.

With Transformational Leadership into New Working Worlds
I have now taken the liberty of taking the model of transformational leadership and transforming it so that it can function for initiatives on new working environments (Fig. 1.2). Because for the preparation of new work settings, a deeper look into the recommendations for action is needed.

---

[4] Pelz, W. Transformationale Führung: Vorteile und Wirkung (neue Studie). Available at: https://www.transformationale-fuehrung.com/index.html.

1 Leadership and New Worlds of Work

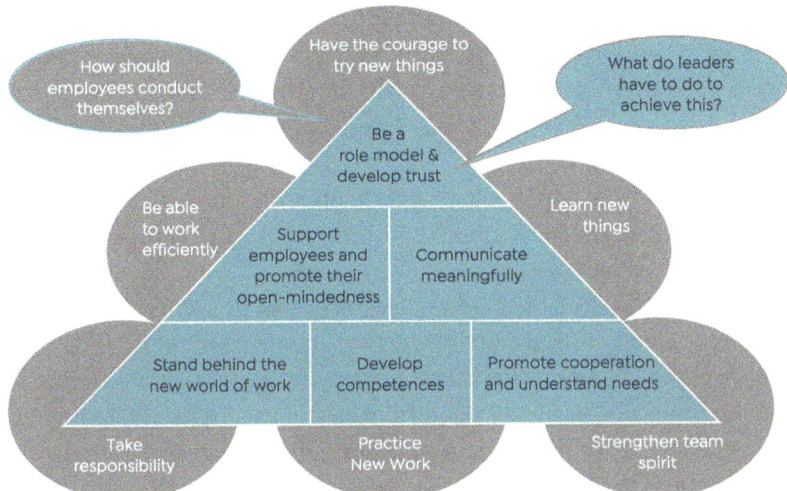

Fig. 1.2 Model of transformational leadership in new work environments. The model shows which competences and behaviours employees need to develop in order to work efficiently in new work environments and how managers need to act to foster them (Gauer Consulting)

The basic prerequisite for this is that everyone gets out of their comfort zone. Because workplace change projects are profound and emotional. They differ significantly from other change initiatives.

The diagram clearly shows how multi-layered a transformational leadership style is in new working environments. I will now start at the employee level, with what you want to achieve as a leader, or I will even go one step further and say what you should achieve. Here, too, I would like to point out once again that it has to be a togetherness on which all behaviours are built.

But before I delve deeper into the individual elements of transformational leadership in new work environments, I would like to make a short excursion to the base camp of workplace initiatives.

What Are the Core Elements that Leaders Should Consider (Fig. 1.3)?
These are so important because they are the basis for all further attempts to reach the summit of the new world of work without perishing from lack of oxygen. Believe me, workplace change initiatives can also be a borderline challenge.

The be-all and end-all for managers at all levels of the hierarchy is that the workplace initiative is aligned with the respective company with its culture, identity and orientation.

Authentic and credible leading *into* new working environments and leadership *in* new working environments can only really work if the superiors are actually behind this initiative and are actively involved, in a targeted manner, in a timely manner and in the right level of detail. Otherwise, we are in the dilemma of honest signals, which I then describe in the chapter "Iceberg Model".

The best concepts are of no use if they do not critically question working methods and working models and adapt them in such a way that they can also be well and meaningfully integrated into the new working world.

Active listening and continuous development are important elements, because I always point out how important it is not to believe that the project is finished with the move into a new working environment. On the contrary, the workplace change really starts then and that is why it is important to grow into it. To achieve this, one has to listen and get involved.

And then it's about the freedom to develop and to allow the employees the same process.

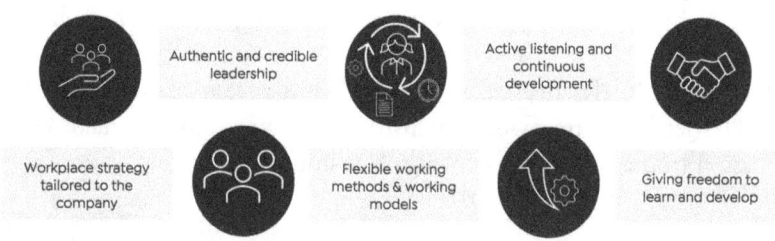

Fig. 1.3 Core features of leadership in new working environments (Gauer Consulting)

Behaviour of Employees (Fig. 1.2)
Have the courage to try new things

People always have an uneasy feeling when they need to leave the familiar. Because it means getting involved in a new environment and a new (working) world. This is unsettling and takes away stability. Especially in times like we are experiencing at the moment, we reach even more for the known and the familiar.

Learn new things

To be able to actually work well in new working environments and to use all the new possibilities that such a new concept offers, it is incredibly important to learn how to handle it. This is because new working environments sometimes fundamentally and profoundly change previous philosophies. It is important to get involved as early as possible in order to benefit from the "early adopter" bonus.

Strengthen team spirit

When working environments become more transparent, they provide much more insight into all processes and sensitivities, as well as communication styles. In order to be prepared for new forms of work, it is important that a team strengthens itself and helps each other. A new "we" form emerges as the individual becomes more transparent. This process should not be underestimated, neither as an employee nor as a manager.

Practice New Work

It is also important to know what New Work actually is. Everyone is talking about it, but it's hard to say exactly what it means. The Zukunftsinstitut describes the megatrend New Work as a fundamentally changed understanding of work and the influence of modern worlds and digitalisation. The boundaries between life and work are blurring in everyday life in a productive manner. In the future, the term work will represent all paid and unpaid activities in different phases of life.[5]

Well, many people already get dizzy just reading that. That is why it is important to define one's own New Work, one's own new working world—in the company, at management level and in teams. It's a wonderful opportunity, but also a challenge.

---

[5] Block, J., Boeing, N., Briegleb, T., Dettling, D., Gatterer, H., Horx, M. (Eds.), Horx, T., Kibala, J., Pfuderer, N., Reichel, A., Schuldt, C., Tewes, S., Wolf, M. Zukunftsreport 2023. 2022.

Take responsibility

This topic has been around for a long time, but due to the many failed attempts and protracted efforts, I have come to the conclusion that it really is not that simple. Where does responsibility begin and where does it end? Who tells me how much responsibility I can take on? Who helps me to shoulder this responsibility? These are fundamental questions and all of them have a claim to leadership support.

Be able to work efficiently

That is almost the output of all behavioural patterns. And yet it fails time and again because employees and even managers know far too little about how to work or lead efficiently in new work environments. It is not something that is going to develop on its own or that can be done quickly. Or as I regularly hear: "It's only a move and then we'll have a beautifully furnished working environment!"

It is much more than just a move, it is a whole new working world with different premises and different ways of doing things. It is a great opportunity, but you have to work for it.

Behaviour of Managers (Fig. 1.2)

Leaders have another inner part in the concept of transformational leadership.

Be a role model and develop trust

As I mentioned earlier, authenticity is the most important asset people have, because it enables them to stay in their own centre and to communicate honestly. Again, I would like to refer you to the section on honest signals later in the book. Trust is a very delicate process and sometimes it does not take much to lose it. Not to mention the trust you have in yourself. I often see managers in particular being pushed into roles and functions they cannot or do not want to take on. This is particularly noticeable in workplace change projects, as this is already an emotional change process.

Again, it is important to know who you are, where you have come from and where you are going. These are very personal questions that often only you can answer. It doesn't matter what the answer is, as long as it comes from a place of deep conviction.

1 Leadership and New Worlds of Work

Communicate meaningfully

This is a topic I am confronted with again and again, and I still do not understand what basic mistakes are made in communication. From lay people (managers) to professionals (communication department). It is sometimes hard to watch. In communication, it is enormously important to inform or communicate with the right target group at the right time and in the right level of detail. It is simple and straightforward, but in many cases it just does not seem to be feasible. People themselves feel that they are communicating correctly and well, and then wonder why the rumour mill or the well-known grapevine is literally overflowing with inconsistent information.

Promote cooperation and understand needs

Oh yes, that is the next big stumbling block to watch out for. Because needs are always an interesting thing. I always say that two ears and one mouth were not given to us humans for nothing. So that we can listen well and, ideally, listen even more than we say. But unfortunately, it is often the other way round, we say a lot and do not listen. This can quickly become a big problem, especially in new working environments.

Because suddenly different groups do not feel heard or represented. And I can confirm that this is often the case. It is often the case that there are pseudo-communication events or e-mails just for the sake of communication. Or that managers will mention in passing that there is a new initiative that will change the working environment, but that it is just a move anyway. As a manager, you are more likely to be tempted to go for the quick win than to climb the mountain in an arduous way. But believe me, if you manage to get up there and take your team with you, listen to their needs and discuss them openly, you will have a view that will stay in your heart and be emotionally positive, which in turn will create a lot of valuable impulses.

Develop competences

The new world of work presents us with many challenges. It is not a question of whether this is the case or not—because it is. It is more a question of what skills I can contribute to ensure that these new working worlds work and do not become a conceptual shelf warmer?

To do this, it is important to first look at your own competencies and see where you stand when it comes to how you see and approach to the new world of work. If you don't do this short self-analysis, it will be difficult to transfer the necessary competencies to your employees. And yes, external consultants can do a lot, but the basic team leadership skills for the new working environment have to be transported and partly transformed by the managers themselves.

Support the new world of work

This is one of the most difficult areas. On the one hand, this is due to the dual role of managers in this field. On the other hand, it is often the case that one is not as well informed, oriented and integrated oneself. And that is where the dilemma already begins. It is important to actively involve all target groups. Here too, the motto "less is more" applies: do not involve everyone on the so-called "watering can principle" but select the appropriate groups in a targeted way. The ability to stand behind the new working worlds authentically is a prerequisite for successful implementation.

Support employees and promote their open-mindedness

Open to the new world of work and the process of change that goes with it. This undertaking builds on all the areas described above. I know how simple and easy this sentence sounds, and I know how difficult it is to implement. What is important is that managers are active creators in this process, not just passive consumers.

And by that I do not mean that everyone should immediately go into operational hectic, even on a small scale one can shape things if the situation or the personalities involved need it this way.

2

New Work Environments: A Strategic Process

2.1 In the Beginning Was the Thought

In the beginning there is always the first thought, the first idea that you want to change something (Fig. 2.1). To be more modern, to be cooler, to be like the others, to use space more efficiently, to have a nicer office, to have agile ways of working and spatial structures, etc. There are many possible ideas that can be the start of a journey into new working worlds.

The initiation of new working environments is a very complex process, which is unfortunately completely underestimated, because it has very far-reaching consequences.

Vision, Strategy and Leadership
Where does the vision come from and how do we know if it is the right one for the organisation? Which of the many possibilities is the most promising for our company? Unfortunately, this question is often given too little attention, but it determines the real and lasting success of new world of work initiatives.

In Fig. 2.1, I have tried to summarise these thoughts and show the dual role of the leader.

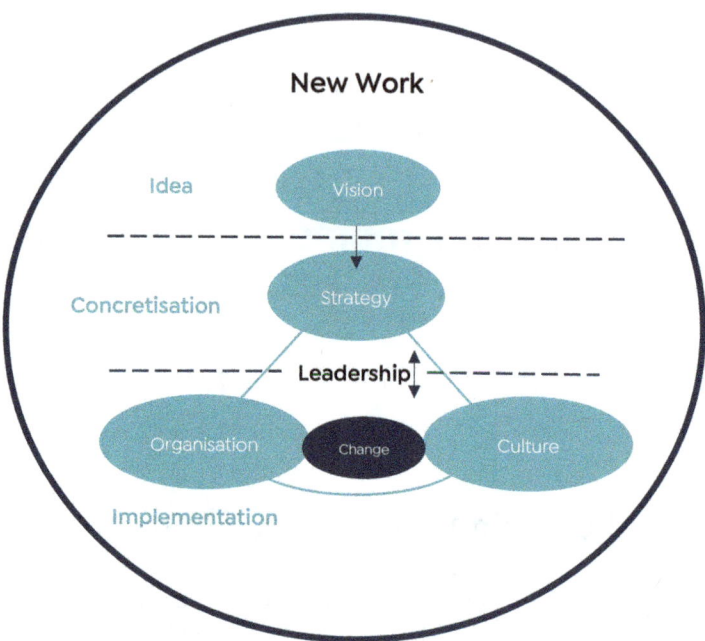

Fig. 2.1 Vision, strategy and leadership. New work environments—from the vision to the product and the dual role of leadership (Gauer Consulting)

2.2 Recognising and Disentangling Complexity

New working environments with their variety of possibilities in open space, multi-space, combi-offices or classic structures have one thing in common: they need a clear strategy and a clear assignment of what a company wants to achieve with this working environment.

For years, the trend in office concepts has been to do what everyone else is doing, and like lemmings, everyone has followed everyone else in the hope of finding their own office truth. They have tried to copy working environments and implement initiatives either with stylish layouts or with well-calculated space efficiency. This worked well until it became clear that the parameters of performance, satisfaction and health were not so easy to integrate.

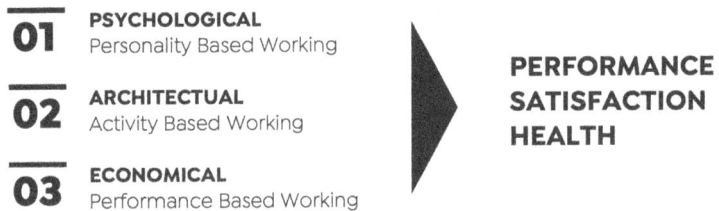

Fig. 2.2 Integration of psychological, architectural and psychological aspects in the design of new working environments to promote performance, satisfaction and health (Gauer Consulting)

It is becoming increasingly clear that people need to be the focus (Fig. 2.2). I do not mean "employee first", where every wish is read from the eyes, which is also a trend at the moment. I mean a balance between human needs and business objectives—a win-win situation, so to speak.

Two aspects need to be taken into account:

1) We need to combine the economic, architectural and psychological aspects in office concepts and the resulting working environments (Fig. 2.2) and integrate them into our actions, and this is already in the stages of strategy and planning.
2) We need to see leadership as a supportive and demanding supporter of the respective new working world, which is allowed to be human and authentic in its form—with its strengths and weaknesses.

2.3 Consider Different Levels

Modern working environments are complex and multi-layered, as several levels come together. Until now, planners and architects have mainly worked on the visible level when designing new working environments. There is a widespread belief that functional space planning, accompanied by cool layouts and fancy furniture, automatically and naturally supports employee performance and a positive management culture. In fact, given the planning and often financial investment involved, people almost feel like they *have* to feel comfortable in the new working environments. Creativity, performance and leadership culture are supposed to be created by the staff at the push of a button, because the company has paid a lot for them.

My many years of experience and well-founded scientific knowledge have shown that spatial worlds are not just layouts, but also consist of the human psyche. We human beings are much more complex than can be explained and simply implemented with spatial structures and design elements.

Knowing this, we have taken a different approach and integrated the partially visible and invisible elements into our work. The illustration below demonstrates this way of thinking.

Workspaces are an agile interplay between the obvious and the hidden. The boundaries between the partially visible and the invisible are fluid and constantly merge, depending on the task at hand.

2.4 The Iceberg Model by Gauer

The Iceberg Model developed by Gauer Consulting (Fig. 2.3) is intended to illustrate the interplay described above.

But let us start with a component of new working environments that is essential to analyse before moving to the visible level—strategy.

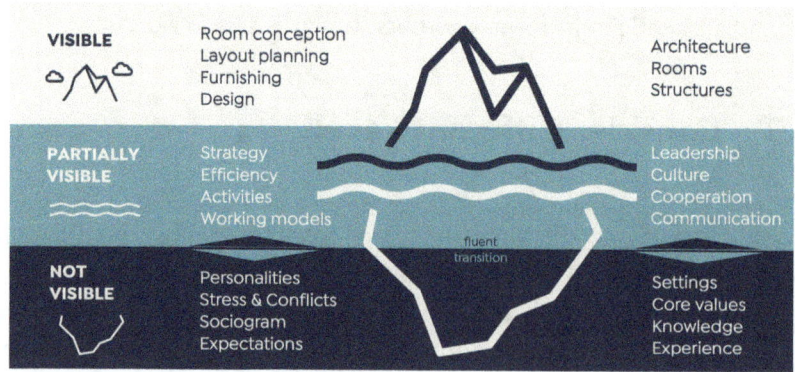

Fig. 2.3 The Iceberg Model. The model shows the multi-layered nature and complexity of new working environments through differently visible levels, which need to be taken into account in initiatives to introduce new working environments (Gauer Consulting)

2 New Work Environments: A Strategic Process

In my experience, when it comes to planning new workspaces, the strategic focus of such far-reaching initiatives is often lacking. New workspace initiatives are still very much in demand, but very often there is a lack of detailed consideration. There is a crucial advantage in being clear about what you want to achieve with a new working environment. The consequences of these decisions and the major implications are underestimated. The fact is that this examination of the issue, or rather of this complex of issues, is already the first decisive factor for success in management.

The more intensively and concertedly management deals with this reorientation, the better the planning and implementation can be. This applies not only to the working world itself, but also to the way in which it is introduced.

In this sensitive phase, it is important to develop your own strategy and to question it at the same time. There are many reasons for introducing new working environments, some of which are very different and require different approaches. It is also important to get the right people involved in these project initiatives to avoid conflicts of resources, skills and objectives. A well-thought-out strategy at the beginning of a project can greatly reduce project and management errors.

Fundamental questions need to be addressed:

1) What are new working worlds for us?
2) What do we want to achieve with this?
3) How much do we need/want to challenge our corporate culture?
4) What kind of working world do we like, and what kind actually suits us?
5) What are the implications of this new working environment for us?
6) How can we, as management teams at different hierarchical levels, successfully support this project?
7) What are the success factors and where are the risks?
8) How brave do we want to be?

The first objective of this strategic phase is to get a clear picture of what new working environments need to achieve and fulfil for the company.

The second objective of this strategic phase is to have a clear picture of what the company needs to achieve and fulfil for new working environments.

Let us now look more closely at the Iceberg Model I have developed.

The Visible Layer Is the Simplest Layer
This level (Fig. 2.4) has been the focus for a very long time and still is. Not that it is unimportant, in fact it is very crucial. Architecture, with its spatial structure, has an enormous influence on layout planning and design. But it would be too short-sighted to define oneself solely in terms of these outward appearances.

Working environments represent an attitude and a way of working, they shape the culture and influence if we work efficiently or not. They play a crucial role in whether you feel comfortable or not. And feeling comfortable does not mean that an office needs to look like your living room at home. In fact, I would advise against it, because we consciously look for variety and the well-known term "change of scenery". More than that, we need it to work efficiently.

I can explain this very well with an example. A very large client of mine called me in because employee satisfaction in their new building was at a mysterious low. They simply could not explain it because the building had been designed by a famous star architect. Everything was perfectly styled. However, the employee survey scores were still way down and one of the main reasons was that the acoustics were perceived to be totally inadequate and people felt distracted all the time. A lot of clear statements from the staff. The case seemed clear, design flaws …

Yes, they were planning mistakes, but not the ones you would think, it was so much more complex and far-reaching. You could say they created the bill without the host.

VISIBLE	Room conception Layout planning Furnishing Design		Architecture Rooms Structures

Fig. 2.4 The visible layer of working environments (Gauer Consulting)

What happened next? I got an acoustician from Berlin to independently check whether it was actually an acoustic problem, because in my opinion, this dissatisfaction had absolutely nothing to do with the classic noise level. The building also spoke against it because it was well planned and thought through.

So, what was it? The reasons, as I discovered in a series of interviews and workshops, were simple, though complex to resolve. The employees did not identify with the building and the spatial structures.

I sat down with the project team and the star architect and tried to build a bridge from them to the staff. It went so far that the client was not even allowed to choose the bouquet of flowers without consultation because it might not fit into the design concept. The staff told me that the building and the architecture, both inside and out, had nothing to do with their history, culture and needs, and that they were never involved in the process in a way that would have allowed them to make a real contribution. Instead, they were limited to pseudo and symbolic change management exercises. The "bad acoustics" were nothing more than a placeholder for absolute dissatisfaction, not only with the process itself, but also with the outcome.

And that brings me to the next level.

The Partially Visible Level

This is where things get a bit more complicated. This part of my Iceberg Model is more on the interpersonal level, but it still has a strong connection and dependency on the concept of space (Fig. 2.5).

When planning spaces, it is essential to first analyse how people work in this company and what culture they live in their company. What values and customs are important and how communication works.

Fig. 2.5 The partially visible layer of working environments (Gauer Consulting)

Management style is an important part of the successful implementation of new working environments. But to ensure this, it is important to present the actual situation and create a basis for discussion.

Time and again, managers tell me that they want to work differently in the new office concept and that they don't need an analysis of the current situation. But that would be like wanting to change and add to a dish without really knowing how to cook it. You can only deal with new requirements efficiently and sensibly if you know where the company is coming from and what is and is not possible in the end. Having the courage to think outside the box, but at the same time knowing where it would be a step too far. The transformation to new working environments is a very complex, difficult and, above all, very emotional process. This change is massively underestimated by companies, which increasingly leads to problems in the implementation of such initiatives.

Working models and activities need to be critically questioned in order to create a meaningful spatial concept and to align them with the strategy for new working environments. Unfortunately, this is something I come across very often in my client projects—many companies want to focus exclusively on the conception of the office space and not on the change and modernisation of the working world as a whole. The term "new working environment" is then usually used only for the office and not for the various dimensions it takes to turn a concept into a successful work environment.

The Titanic was also thought to be unsinkable and then sank because of this exact iceberg. To rephrase this a little more strikingly, I have simply found that many companies are too late in realising the many dimensions of new working environments and the many pitfalls that lie like a minefield along the way.

This brings me to the last level, which I think is the most exciting.

The Invisible Layer in the Iceberg Model

And this is where it gets really exciting, even adventurous, and that is not even an exaggeration. For it is at this level (Fig. 2.6) that all the emotional processes take place that make workplace change initiatives so challenging and cross-disciplinary.

2 New Work Environments: A Strategic Process 21

Fig. 2.6 The invisible layer of working environments (Gauer Consulting)

In order to achieve really good results and create working environments that are successful in the long term, it is essential to get down to the human level. To look at the world that does not immediately jump out at us but can be the jumping-off point for failure. I do not mean wishful thinking and playing Santa Claus but understanding human behaviour and responding to it appropriately. This is not a job for architects and designers, but for psychologists, and architectural psychologists to be precise. It is about how we behave in spaces and how spaces affect our experiences and feelings.

We cannot escape this effect, so it is more about how we can make the most of it.

Many workplace change projects fail or do not reach their potential because this invisible layer is at the heart of the initiative. For everyone involved, from the project member to the employee. Our attitudes, values, experiences and personalities play a critical role in how successful these initiatives are. Money is usually invested in the visible level of space design and not in the people who work in it. But, as I mentioned at the beginning, it is about the behaviour of people in spaces and what different working environments trigger in people, depending on their disposition.

But to be able to actively support as a leader, it is important that you yourself are aware of the complexity. This transformation process does not work alone in most cases.

Managers need clear support that is tailored to new working environments. In my projects, I often find that people think that one to two workshops are enough to get things under control. After all, there is no magic, my God, a move to a fancy office, what is there to change?

It starts with managers being so busy with to-dos that they stop listening. I have an example that illustrates this beautifully. I was doing a workshop with a client's managers and I asked them some questions via an online tool that they had to answer on their laptops. What the managers did not know was that in addition to what I was saying, I was simply observing their behaviour. And it was exactly as I had predicted.

My question was: "Can you listen well and wait until your counterpart has finished telling his story?" Good listening skills are very important, especially for managers, and are even mentioned in every management book. It is not for nothing that evolution gave us two ears and one mouth, it is essential for survival—not only in the past, but still today. Although it is no longer so much a matter of physical survival.

Now, you may be wondering what has come of my little leadership experiment. The answer is simple. No one really listened. How did I know?

While I was asking the question, it was simultaneously being displayed. I specifically asked people to listen to what I had to say until the end and then click. What happened? Around 95 per cent of the participants—there were 25 of them—had already clicked while I was talking. Of that 95 per cent, the vast majority said they listened very well and a few said they listened well. When I asked at the end what I had said, only the 5 per cent who had really waited until the end could repeat it.

Why am I telling this story?

New working environments are so much more than mere spatial concepts, because they require our focus and absolute concentration, as they literally change the world in which we move. For managers in particular, this concentration and focus can sometimes be a decisive factor, because they have to play a double role. On the one hand, they are affected employees themselves and, on the other hand, they have to provide help and support when this process of change begins. But the way in which managers involve their employees is also crucial. Very often we see that there is a conflict of resources, i.e. there is no time to really deal with this new world of work, there are so many other things to do that are more important. The awareness is not there at all, and even if it were, I have often observed that there is no time to really focus on it.

Unfortunately, this is also a social problem, but the working world is to some extent a reflection of our society, with all its strengths and weaknesses. The manager is supposed to be an active player in this, but often becomes an extra.

But again, going back to the invisible layer of the Iceberg Model, there is also a strong dependence of the behaviour of managers on their attitudes, values, experiences and personalities. Unfortunately, the impact of new work environments on people is still underestimated, and why it is so important to know people as people before designing spaces for them. Understanding human psychology and translating it into architecture is the key and the real secret of success.

As I mentioned at the beginning, the Titanic sank even though it was thought to be unsinkable. Our working worlds are not dissimilar to the Titanic, just like then, people believe that size and grandeur outshine everything and are a guarantee of success for that reason alone. Well, you might want to read up on history.

2.5 What Does this Mean for Leadership?

2.5.1 For Managers

Leadership in modern working environments means developing the ability to link the different levels again and again and to move between the different levels again and again.

To disentangle the complexity for oneself and to find one's own access codes for true authenticity and resilience. The problem of our time is that we want everything and preferably immediately. We live in a massiveness that is sometimes hard to bear. But above all, it alienates us from ourselves. Our motto in recent years has been: More is more—but the motto for the next few years should be: Less is more.

More humility and authenticity again. Unfortunately, the art of "being oneself" is only given to a few and modesty is also a nice buzzword to swear us into being fully trendy in business life. The more we try to appear genuine, the less we are. The art of re-exploring the levels of our personality, needs and fears honestly and with an open heart will help us answer questions and recognise possibilities.

New worlds of work give us the chance to define new real worlds, because for the first time in the history of modern work we have the opportunity to live our inner freedom and to really implement what we want and who we are. But first we have to know what we need.

2.5.2 For Employees

There are very few people who can be authentic on their own. Our societal constraints are too strong, and also the fact that we have more and more time to think about things, but we do not use this time constructively enough for ourselves. This can be by always being the closest to ourselves or by always wanting to please everyone else. Often there is a lack of healthy selfishness. Some have too much of it, others too little—a perpetual dilemma.

The skills shortage also plays into our hands to a certain extent, sometimes in a less than ideal way. As a manager, you often have the feeling that you have to keep the employee at all costs, and the trend of "We apply to the potential employees" has also arrived in HR departments.

Psychologically, however, we need to be sincere to make a lasting difference. We need to be fair but clear about what we want and not be afraid to ask for it. Encouraging and demanding are like yin and yang—you need both.

2.6 Building New Working Environments in a Meaningful Way

In all the years that I have been working as a consultant for new working environments, it has become clear to me that office architecture is not only a design topic for future working environments, but that the existing spaces are an important indicator and thus also a sensitive diagnostic tool to analyse the "state" in a company beyond all verbalisations and self-proclamations, to plan and then to implement it according to the needs of the company and its employees.

The office as a central factor has not been underestimated in recent years, in fact a lot of money has been invested. However, from my point of view, the actual potential and the underlying problems have been wrongly assessed and thus structures, designs and layout variants have been created that do not correspond to people and their needs. At the end of the day, it is not about these fancy worlds, it is about the human image and the lifestyles of our society that lie behind them. It is about the human being with his original and not learned needs, which are more hidden in us than a superficial view would show.

2.6.1 Recognising Potentials

The aim is to create new working environments in a meaningful way and to take account of their individual characteristics. Small and medium-sized enterprises have different needs and possibilities than large companies. It is important that the respective requirements for a modern, efficient and flexible working environment are covered and matched with the needs of the employees and the possibilities of the company.

2.6.2 Actively Involving Employees

Active, authentic and credible employee involvement is essential for the successful implementation of new working environments. However, it is important that involvement is meaningful and does not lead to actionism or pseudo-involvement. The right target group, at the right time, with the right level of detail. This is how you can successfully manage ongoing collaboration throughout the project.

2.6.3 Enabling Leadership

Leadership in new office structures is a key success factor in turning an office concept into a vibrant, sustainable and inclusive working environment. It is important not to deprive managers of their power and to see them as this essential building block that they form.

2.6.4 Designing the Office According to Needs

New working environments are the result of a coordinated chain of decision-making and planning. It is important, on the one hand, to let the formulation of needs flow into an architectural-psychological design and, on the other hand, to enable a translation into an office layout (Fig. 2.7).

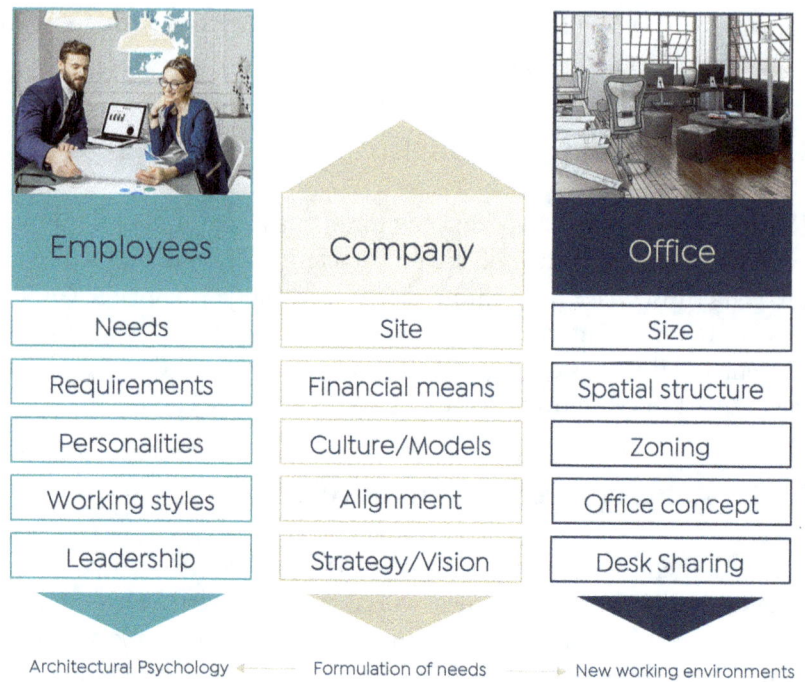

Fig. 2.7 Designing the office according to needs (Gauer Consulting)

2.7 Human Resources and the New World of Work

2.7.1 Corporate Values as a Driving Force

Organisational values are the main driver of flexibility and agility in multi-space offices and a determining force in shaping the social climate in a company. Organisational values are also the basis on which the collective sense of the organisation emerges and provide guidance for the actions and behaviour of employees.[1]

Values ensure the coherence of collective action and provide a framework for evaluating the behaviour of others. They enable collective change and are of great strategic importance, especially when organisations need

---

[1] Williams, S. Strategic planning and organizational values: links to alignment. Human Resource Development International. 2002;5(2):217–233.

to adapt to rapidly changing markets and environments. The strategic importance of HR and HR management is increasingly reflected in the formulation of strategic decisions for organisations. Not only are organisations recognising that they need to change due to technological or market pressures, but they are also recognising that the people who are faced with these changes need to adapt quickly.[2]

Multi-space offices and the division of space into functional areas reflect changing market and technology dynamics. People working in these functional areas need to adapt their behaviour accordingly to meet both the changing dynamics and the potential of Activity-Based Working (ABW). And then there are the personality factors. Not every employee will integrate the same way into the different zones of agile and flexible working.

2.7.2 Interaction Between Manager and Human Resources Department

It is now the responsibility not only of managers but also of HR to guide and direct the development of employees and their culture. Adapting employees to the usability of multi-space offices thus becomes a goal embedded in larger cultural initiatives within the organisation. The way organisations work is reflected in the physical space. For example, there is evidence that an innovative and collaborative climate can lead to an increase in social interactions,[3] or that mutual trust, flat hierarchies or open feedback cultures promote stronger teamwork.[4]

In order to promote leadership in multi-space offices and ensure the flexibility of these spaces, HR practices also need to be designed from a perspective that considers values as the fulcrum of any cultural change. These values then need to be translated into concrete measures and

---

[2] Hassan, A. Human resource development and organizational values. Journal of European Industrial Training. 2007;31(6):435–448.

[3] E.g. Chen, C., Huang, J. How organizational climate and structure affect knowledge management—The social interaction perspective. Internationale Zeitschrift für Informationsmanagement, 2007;27(2):104–118. DOI: 10.1016/j.ijinfomgt.2006.11.001.

[4] Haner, U., Wackernagel, S. Kurzbericht zur Studie. Wirksame Büro- und Arbeitswelten. Ausgewählte Erfolgsfaktoren für eine wirksame Gestaltung von Büro- und Arbeitswelten. 2018. Available at: http://publica.fraunhofer.de/dokumente/N-494183.html.

actions, such as leadership training, learning and development programmes or recruitment strategies.[5]

Values are the fuel and initiatives the vehicle for change. Cultural change and the reformulation of values must not only be promised but put into practice and sustained at all levels of the organisation through appropriate development programmes and support structures.

When we talk about values as tools for creating affective attachment to an organisation, we are referring to human values such as courtesy, cooperation and respect, as well as visionary values such as development, openness and creativity. These values can promote secure attachment styles to the workplace and the organisation, because, on the one hand, personal and creative development is supported and, on the other hand, the organisation and the workplace as its physical embodiment provide a more human and supportive atmosphere.[6]

Since flexibility, the dynamic and satisfaction with the multi-space office depend to a large extent on the emotional climate created by employees, the quality of leadership in new work environments is determined to a substantial extent by the ability of managers to access employees' emotions.

Emotional information can be understood as a set of signals that provide information about how the individual assesses phenomena that are important for survival, such as perceived threats, conflict, appeasement, alliances, etc.[7] On the other hand, emotional intelligence is understood by Mayer, Salovey and Caruso as "the capacity to reason about emotions, and of emotions to enhance thinking […] which includes the abilities to accurately perceive emotions, to access and generate emotions so as to assist thought, to understand emotions and emotional knowledge, and to reflectively regulate emotions so as to promote emotional and intellectual growth".[8]

---

[5] Williams, S. Strategic planning and organizational values: links to alignment. Human Resource Development International. 2002;5(2):217–233.

[6] Finegan, J. The impact of person and organizational values on organizational commitment. Journal of Occupational and Organizational Psychology. 2000;73(2):149–169.

[7] Mayer, J.D., Salovey, P., Caruso, D.R. Emotional intelligence: Theory, findings and implications. Psychological Inquiry. 2004;15(3):197–215.

[8] Mayer, J.D., Salovey, P., Caruso, D.R. Emotional intelligence: Theory, findings and implications. Psychological Inquiry. 2004;15(3):197.

3

New Working Environments Create Stress

3.1 Positive and Negative Stress

In a way, eustress can be seen as a good form of stress that we need to keep our inner engine at operating temperature. It drives us (in conjunction with other physical and mental stimuli) to come up with new ideas in the office, to complete tasks well and quickly, or to perform well in sport. Stress can therefore motivate us to perform and pursue a task in a focused and efficient manner (Fig. 3.1). So, to be productive and challenging, you need a healthy amount of positive stress. Eustress therefore helps us to "stay on the ball".

We know from evolutionary biology that we still live in fight or flight mode. Although we do not like to hear it, and may not even be aware of it, our programmes still run as they did in the old days. In the face of danger, we can either attack or flee. In a matter of seconds, we have to assess the situation and act. The stress level rises massively, adrenaline is pumped into the body at lightning speed and then it starts…

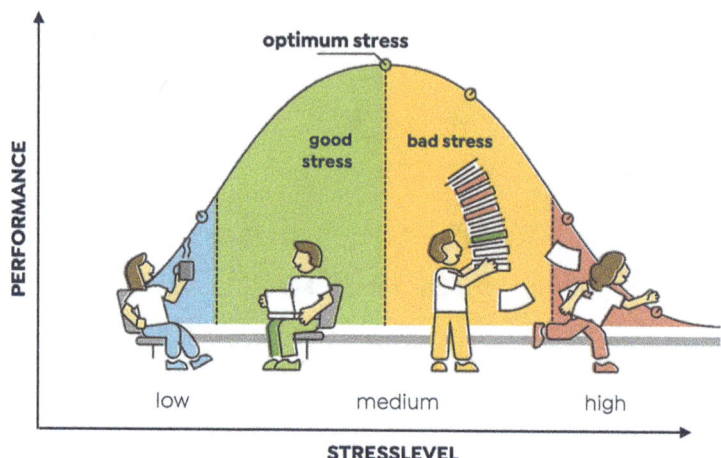

Fig. 3.1 The stress curve. A certain level of stress can promote motivation and performance (Gauer Consulting)

3.2 Acting in an Evolutionary-Biological Yet Socially Correct Way

But where does it begin nowadays? This is the big question of our time. What are we allowed to do in order to remain socially acceptable? It is becoming more and more difficult to act, because we have to go through far too many evaluation patterns in order to come to an action. We literally have to make an intuitive checklist of what is socially desirable and what is not. Are we being "woke" enough? Are we too masculine? Or even too feminine? Are we excluding someone through our behaviour? Are we harking back too much to the past? Are we too conservative? Are we too progressive?

This list is enough to make you dizzy. And many processes of flight and fight take place in the unconscious part of our perception. This means that we are almost fighting against evolutionary biology, because we can no longer act in the way that is written in our genetic make-up. This makes things even more complicated.

3 New Working Environments Create Stress

This new situation is also one of the reasons why stress and burnout have risen massively in recent years and continue to do so. This is now also happening to young people who have their whole working lives ahead of them. We have, to a certain extent, lost mediocrity and are trapped in our own illusory world.

Our stress levels are rising because we are living in uncertain times and we can no longer cope constructively with the tasks involved in our professional and private lives, resulting in massive distress.

Negative stress occurs as soon as we feel overwhelmed. This often happens insidiously, we do not notice immediately how strong the stress level really is. When we do realise it, it can be frustrating because there is no foreseeable solution to the task at hand. When we do realise it, it can be frustrating because there is no foreseeable solution to the task at hand.

Physical effects of this type of stress can include high blood pressure, digestive problems, a rise in blood sugar levels, irregular/shallow breathing and the development of allergies or skin irritations (Fig. 3.2). Behavioural symptoms may include loss of appetite, food cravings, listlessness or fatigue.

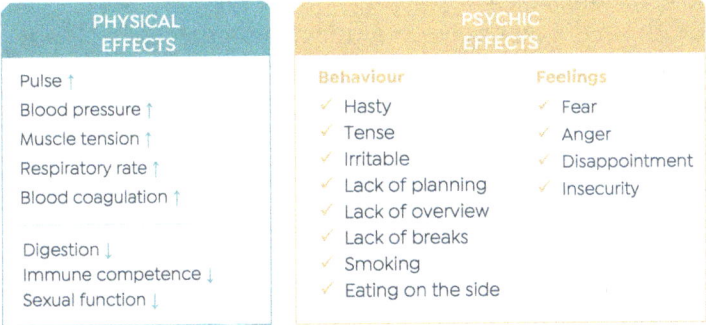

Fig. 3.2 Possible physical and psychological consequences of negative stress (Gauer Consulting)

3.3 The Office as a Risk Area: A Development

Looking back over the past two and a half years, the picture is clear: The stressors that surround us are of crisis proportions, with devastating economic, financial and health consequences. We are becoming more and more of a service society, lulling ourselves into a false sense of security.

Fewer and fewer people are working in high-risk sectors such as construction or industry, which, in combination with other factors, has led to a significant reduction in work-related accidents in recent years. According to the Swiss Accident Insurance Fund (UVG), the risk of occupational accidents has fallen by 45 per cent since 1985. The risk of a fatal accident at work has fallen by as much as 60 per cent.[1]

Safe office, dangerous industry? But it is not all that simple. There are other dangers lurking in the office, dangers that have been underestimated for years and that also have a strong impact on leadership opportunities and leadership qualities.

The problem is not physical but psychological. And the figures speak a clear language: Work absences due to mental illness reached a new high in 2022. Work incapacity as a result of mental illness has also risen sharply between 2012 and 2022.[2]

The Corona pandemic has made the situation much worse. The dilemma should not be underestimated. With the shortage of skilled workers due to the baby boomers retiring, the bottleneck is already intensifying out of a natural problem, and when the health failures of the next generation come on top of that, then the shit hits the fan.

---

[1] Koordinationsgruppe für die Statistik der Unfallversicherung UVG (KSUV) c/o SUVA. Unfallstatistik UVG 2022. 2022.

[2] DAK. Psychreport 2023. Entwicklungen der psychischen Erkrankungen im Job: 2012–2022. 2023. Available at: https://caas.content.dak.de/caas/v1/media/32628/data/3983614e98a936fe7d7dd70f3dac2e73/dak-psychreport-ergebnis-praesentation.pdf.

3.4 The Stressors Right in Front of you

By creating different work zones for different activities, multi-space offices encourage mobility. The new dynamics also create new stress factors. On the other hand, the new dynamics of open space and mobility redefine the constellation of spaces that provide privacy. In short, open-space offices promote both the need for privacy and the need for social interaction. This seemingly contradictory statement is justified by the fact that more open office structures "expose" the individual more to the world, but the dynamics of the place reinforce the desire for more social interaction.[3]

This goes hand in hand with the idea of New Work: the workplace is increasingly becoming a place of social interaction. As a result of this new development and the spatial structure, the most frequently reported stressors in open-plan offices are:

- Office noise.[4]
- Reduced privacy[5] and lack of retreat areas.[6]
- Reduced confidentiality.[7]
- Increased disturbance from others.[8]

---

[3] Haans, A., Kaiser, F. G., & de Kort, Y. A. Privacy needs in office environments: Development of two behavior-based scales. European Psychologist. 2007;12(2):93–102.

[4] E.g. Lai, L., Chau, K., Davies, S., Kwan, L. Open space office: A review of the literature and Hong Kong case studies. Work. 2021;28(3):749–758. DOI: 10.3233/WOR-203408.

[5] E.g. Jungsoo, K., de Dear, R. Workplace satisfaction: The privacy-communication trade-off in open-plan offices. Journal of Environmental Psychology. 2013;36:18–26. DOI: 10.1016/j.jenvp.2013.06.007.

[6] Becker, C., Kratzer, N., Lanfer, S. Neue Arbeitswelten: Wahrnehmung und Wirkung von Open-Space-Büros. Arbeit. 2019;28(3):263–284. DOI:10.1515/arbeit-2019-0017.

[7] Ibid.

[8] E.g. Ibid.

- Feeling of depersonalisation and low status.[9]
- Visual distraction.[10]
- Problems with climate/air quality.[11]

These stressors can interfere with the ability to cope with current work demands, which in turn can increase and exacerbate existing stressors and work demands. In general, I have experienced that a low level of privacy can exacerbate the negative effects of stress, while a high level of privacy helps to counteract exhaustion and stress. Of course, this is not a universal concept for all employees.

The occurrence of potential stressors is independent of individual appraisal, but managers need to consider that the appraisal of these stressors is subject to personal appraisal, which is dependent on personal characteristics. On the other hand, stressors in multi-space offices arise mainly from social interactions in an environment that is more dynamic and open than in traditional spaces. This means that stressors can be addressed regardless of the subject and can be reduced by implementing rules at the organisational level. Stressors cause negative emotions in employees and can lead to performance losses at individual and organisational level.

3.5 We Overtake Ourselves

Humans are the result of a long evolution in which a spiritual and cultural development has taken place within a biological framework. Although there are biological imprints, they offer culturally formable scope for action, which is, however, not unlimited. An example of this is the innate aversion to strangers, which is already neurologically detectable in young children.

---

[9] E.g. Morrison, R., Smollan, R. Open plan office space? If you're going to do it, do it right: A fourteen-month T longitudinal case study. Applied Ergonomics. 2019;82:102933. DOI: 10.1016/j.apergo.2019.102933.

[10] E.g. Ibid.

[11] E.g. Becker, C., Kratzer, N., Lanfer, S. Neue Arbeitswelten: Wahrnehmung und Wirkung von Open-Space-Büros. Arbeit. 2019;28(3):263–284. DOI:10.1515/arbeit-2019-0017.

Nevertheless, we have developed the ability to live in harmony with, respect and appreciate people of different ethnicities. However, in times of need, ethnic differences can quickly lead to escalating conflicts. It is significant to understand that the further cultural patterns of behaviour move away from our spontaneous inclinations, the more time-consuming and arduous their acquisition becomes, and the more fragile the pattern becomes. The more our way of life deviates from our natural behaviour and needs, the more fragile and exhausting our life as a whole becomes, and the more often mental disorders occur.

This is another piece of the puzzle that helps to explain why burnout and exhaustion depression have increased enormously in recent years, even though we have more and more modern, beautifully designed and sometimes very expensive office environments. Everything is becoming more open and transparent, people can no longer withdraw and pause for breath. Very often not even at home or in society itself, because it has been shaken up by many events of the recent past. And these things do something to us.

There are an increasing number of reports of crisis situations affecting deeper and deeper levels of our human existence, and at shorter and shorter intervals. So, what can we do?

People need contact with nature and sufficient physical activity. Yet, more and more people are withdrawing into cities or digital worlds, leading to a lack of exercise and an increase in obesity. More and more children are unable to swim or do simple physical activities, leading to neglect of their physical health.

Furthermore, we need to control undesirable aspects of our psyche as much as possible. The human psyche contains behavioural patterns that had survival value in early history, but are counterproductive in our culture today, such as abuse of power and aggressiveness. Throughout history, humanity has tried to evolve, to overcome old patterns and to strengthen self-control.

It is nevertheless important to be cautious in this context as well, as occasional lapses should be tolerated under stressful conditions or in moments of spontaneous exuberance. Striving for complete freedom from error would mean a tiring effort at self-control and ultimately rob one of the joys of life.

3.6 Resilience Also Means Being Realistic

In new working environments, it is important to distinguish between realism and optimism depending on the topic. Resilient individuals are characterised by a sober view of those aspects of reality that are crucial for coping with the challenges in this environment. They do not harbour illusions but are able to distinguish between factors that can be influenced and those that cannot.

From my point of view, we are currently experiencing a form of dialogue in society that is too emotional. We only argue emotionally and not based on the matter at hand. It is dismissed by society as "unwoke" and not socially acceptable. Yet, we need this distinction in order to build resilience sustainably and use it meaningfully for ourselves.

In a changing world of work with all its challenges, it is indeed helpful to promote optimism that focuses on an "it-goes attitude" to motivate a "demoralised" workforce. Nevertheless, maintaining a sober, sometimes almost pessimistic sense of reality is crucial for developing strategies and implementing measures. It is important for me to mention, however, that realism in no way means dramatically exaggerating risks. This is in contrast to the stress type patterns in stress research, which are characterised by hecticness, exaggeration and complaining. Realistic people do not tend to make big disasters out of small problems or talk themselves into stress scenarios. A realistic approach also includes appropriate social comparison.

An example of this would be someone who has an excellent canteen available, but continuously complains about the food or criticises the colours in a meeting bunk instead of the functionality of the facilities. Such reactions are not realistic and yet all of us know them. Have we not?

It has been my experience that, when people talk about change in companies, they talk about it as if it were a disaster in itself. This also has to do—and I have to admit this myself—with change management, which in some cases does not achieve its goals. Many companies believe that anyone can do change management and photography.

But the fact is, and I experience this in every project: new working environments can trigger panic or incomprehension in many people, and it can seem as if they are being forced into these changes against their will.

This has to do with the fact that these kinds of change projects are unfortunately completely underestimated. Whereas elsewhere people are putting the pedal to the metal with fear and panic, workplace change initiatives are massively downplayed. Precisely because people believe that it is either just a moving project or that they will get such a beautiful new working world anyway, they cannot help but be overjoyed and grateful.

From a resilience perspective, however, it is not advisable to keep employees in change processes in the dark about the risks, which is often done with workplace initiatives. Why? Because the project leaders themselves are not aware of the box they are opening. It is inappropriate to mislead them with false reassurance or inaccurate information, or to mislead them into seeing factual disadvantages as opportunities. Leaders should instead encourage their employees with comprehensive information to think outside the box and stay grounded in reality. This is especially crucial in the new world of work. Because the big hammer is coming—we do not have to fool ourselves about that. The question is more, how do we deal with it?

Mostly by preparing for the "worst case" and avoiding downplaying or overestimating risks. Key questions in this context are: Do I really understand the reality of my situation and am I prepared to give up protective assertions and endure negative emotions? Do I know what is expected of me and what demands the situation makes? Do I have realistic expectations or are my demands excessive?

3.7 Dealing with Stressors: The Theory

The management of stressors at work is often discussed in the scientific literature. Two basic stress theories serve as a starting point for this discussion.

On the one hand, the "job-demand-resources model" explains that the health of employees is a balance between job resources and job stress. A negative balance is characterised by high stress and low availability of resources. This can lead to burnout or other negative health outcomes. A positive balance, on the other hand, can lead to greater engagement and improved work performance.[12]

On the other hand, the "transactional stress theory" describes the mental processes that trigger the occurrence of a stressor. Potential stressful situations can be interpreted as a threat, but also as a challenge. A challenge requires the mobilisation of resources but focuses on the growth potential of a situation. A threat, on the other hand, is expected to cause harm. This initial assessment is followed by a second assessment of the feasibility of the situation. Part of this second assessment is to find out what strategies or resources are available to resolve the situation. It also considers whether the means available are appropriate to the situation and the likelihood of achieving the desired outcome. If a situation is considered dangerous and the resources needed to deal with it are not available, this can trigger stress.[13]

3.8 Actively Confronting the Stress Issue

In order to remain efficient and healthy in a flexible working environment, and at the same time meet the demands of a modern society, companies and their ambassadors, the managers, increasingly need to recognise, address and actively work on the problems that arise.

3.9 Dealing with Stressors: An Approach

Based on these assumptions, Gauer Consulting has developed a framework (Fig. 3.3) that combines parts of the aforementioned stress theories with pandemic-related stressors and organisational influences and consequences, thus providing practitioners with an efficient tool.

---

[12] Schaufeli, W. B. & Bakker A. B. Job demands, job resources, and their relationships with burnout and engagement: A multi-sample study, Journal of Organizational Behavior. 2004;25(3):293–315. doi: 10.1002/job.248.
[13] Lazarus R., Folkman S. Stress, Appraisal und Coping. New York: Springer Publishing Company. 1984.

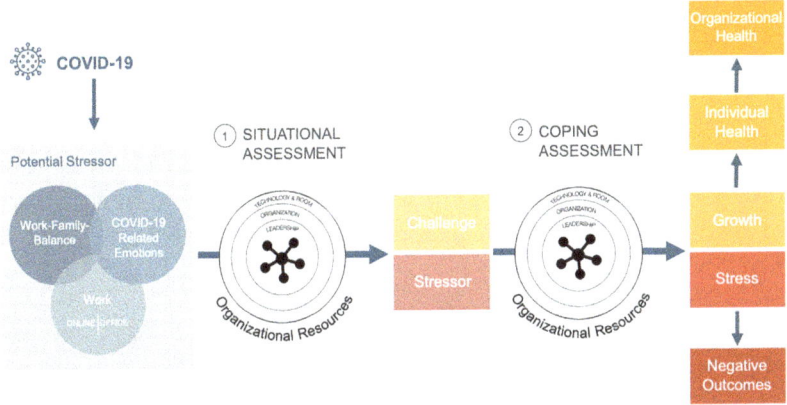

Fig. 3.3 Framework programme of holistic health in companies. A practice-oriented framework programme by Gauer Consulting that combines stress theory and pandemic-related aspects with organisational influences and consequences (Gauer Consulting)

The approach specifies that different stressors can result from the pandemic situation. The personal assessment is, naturally, related to one's own experience, personality, knowledge and attitude. That is why dealing with stressors is individual and cannot be applied to everyone.

Stressors can lead to either positive or negative outcomes, depending on the interpretation of a potentially stressful situation and the possible coping strategies. Specifically, people first assess whether a situation should be interpreted as harmful, i.e. a stressor, or as a challenge. This is usually done intuitively and is, of course, a source of error that should not be underestimated, as we naturally judge according to how we feel. However, it is important to transform this intuitive evaluation into a guided evaluation. This is the only way to determine, in a second step, whether you have the resources to cope with the stressor or challenge.

If so, a situation has the capacity to stimulate personal growth and support personal and organisational health in the long term. If not, a situation is likely to cause stress and lead to negative outcomes such as poor performance or health. Changes at an organisational level, including physical, technical and structural changes, as well as the introduction of coaching or leadership measures, can move both assessment processes in the desired direction.

Concrete Action Steps for Companies

By applying the framework, users gain insight into the implementation of concrete actions (Fig. 3.4). These actions are divided into the following categories: Solutions that affect leaders (micro level), Actions that the organisation can implement (meso level), and Changes in the category "Technology and Space". This places a new focus on technical, spatial and land-based solutions that represent the workplace as the basis for efficient work.

Changes in the Category "Technology and Space"

A functional environment is the foundation for successful work. Whether working from home or in the office, all employees should be well-equipped: with the right hardware, such as powerful laptops and work phones, as well as work-related (e.g. SAP, Microsoft Office, SPSS) or knowledge-related software (e.g. wikis, webinars, e-books).

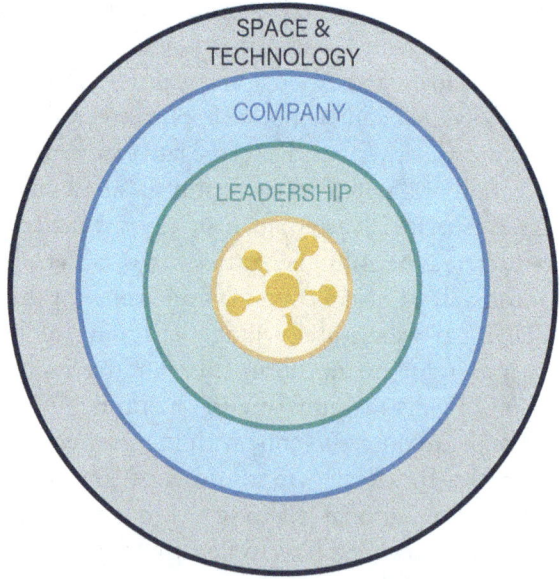

action steps for companies

Fig. 3.4 Concrete action steps for companies based on the framework programme of holistic health in companies (Fig. 3.3) (Gauer Consulting)

3 New Working Environments Create Stress

Communication plays an important role in this category. Email as the primary means of communication is very ineffective and leads to a lot of wasted time. It is therefore worth investing in a comprehensive approach that integrates short phone calls and chat messages into everyday life.

In terms of space, the functional design and active integration of working from home are particularly important. In this context, a company should consider the separation of work and leisure zones, adequate lighting and ergonomic measures.

But there are also many changes that can be made in the office space that not only increase efficiency but also sustainably improve the well-being of employees. The multi-space concept in particular supports different ways of working and innovative work structures: well-being is eight to 18 per cent higher, motivation nine to 17 per cent higher and performance five to 17 per cent higher than in other office forms.[14] In contrast to the open-plan office, the multi-space concept is characterised by great diversity. It consists of individual and group offices as well as social and recreational zones and focus workstations. In addition, employees in a multi-space environment benefit from more retreat zones than in other structures. This may come as a surprise, but the key difference is that retreat zones in multi-space concepts are specifically planned and used. In small structures with mostly one or two person offices, there are few opportunities to signal that you want to concentrate. By sitting at a focus workstation, however, you make it clear that you do not want to be disturbed.

Collaboration also benefits from the multi-space concept: studies show that collaboration in a multi-space is around 6 per cent higher than in a single office.[15] In addition, communication channels are shortened and meeting zones focus on exchange, which in turn improves the efficiency and performance of meetings.

---

[14] Jurecic, M. Gut zu wissen: die Wirkung von Büroumgebungen auf unterschiedliche Arbeitstypen. In S. Wörwag, & A. Cloots (Eds.), Zukunft der Arbeit – Perspektive Mensch. Springer Gabler. 2020:331–340.

[15] Haner U, Wackernagel S. Kurzbericht zur Studie "Wirksame Büro- und Arbeitswelten". Ausgewählte Erfolgsfaktoren für eine wirksame Gestaltung von Büro- und Arbeitswelten. 2018. Available at: http://publica.fraunhofer.de/dokumente/N-494183.html.

Desk sharing is also becoming increasingly important in the context of multi-space. However, many companies use desk sharing with the wrong idea in mind: they try to reduce space in order to save on space costs. It would be better to use the space gained through desk sharing for new multi-space possibilities, for example with additional exchange and retreat zones, in order to offer employees a diverse working environment.

It is important to note that major technological and structural changes also require a rethinking of work processes and collaboration. These changes lead to innovations at higher levels, such as organisational structure and culture, where it is important to adapt the premises to the needs of the employees and the organisation.[16] Change managers therefore need to be involved in larger organisational processes in order to achieve the best possible fit between person and space. The most important premise is therefore Focus on the people, not the space!

3.10 What Does this Mean for Leadership?

Managers face massively changed challenges. The world is changing faster than we can keep up, and this has a huge impact on the world in which we work and live. According to the Job Stress Index, absenteeism due to stress-related stress disorders has increased by 70 per cent in Switzerland between 2013 and 2019. In addition, 30.3 per cent of the working population suffers from exhaustion, and in economic terms we are talking about an annual economic loss of 6.5 billion Swiss francs.[17]

That is an announcement!

We need to look at this development from two perspectives. The demands on leaders have changed enormously; they should no longer be too hierarchically oriented, not too power-hungry, not too know-it-all,

---

[16] Wörwag, S., & Cloots, A. Zukunft der Arbeit – Perspektive Mensch, Springer Fachmedien, Wiesbaden, Germany. 2020.

[17] Galliker, S., Igic, I., Elfering, A. & K Simmer, N. Job-Stress-Index 2022: Monitoring von Kennzahlen zum Stress bei Erwerbstätigen in der Schweiz. (Gesundheitsförderung Schweiz, Eds.). 2022.

not have too high demands on the staff, etc. On the other hand, they should be fair, inclusive, supportive, non-judgemental and have emotional intelligence, etc.

Leaders today must also take full responsibility for the people in their team, as their employees, not just for the work that needs to be done.

4

Discover Efficiency Killers

4.1 Constant Interruptions

It is enormous: 58 billion euros are lost every year alone because employees in knowledge-intensive professions are constantly interrupted in their work.[1]

Studies have shown that there are an average of 15 interruptions per working hour, or one every 4 min. Depending on the complexity of the task, it takes between 15 and 24 percent more time than usual to finish the task. This adds up to three full working days per month lost to interruptions alone.[2]

It is very easy to see this for yourself because every impulse that takes your attention away from what you are doing, whether it is distraction from outside via messenger services or from yourself because you are looking at your phone—these are all interruptions.

It is now empirically proven that the higher the level of digitalisation, the higher the level of fragmentation and stress. This supports the notion that many companies are just collecting tools rather than using them

---

[1] Starker, V., Roos, K., Bracht, E. M., Graudenz, D. Kosten von Arbeitsunterbrechungen für deutsche Unternehmen. Auswirkungen von Fragmentierung auf Produktivität und Stressentwicklung. 2022.

[2] Ibid.

© The Author(s), under exclusive license to Springer Nature Switzerland AG 2024
S. Gauer, *Leadership in New Working Environments*, Business Guides on the Go,
https://doi.org/10.1007/978-3-031-50434-1_4

wisely. For example, chat applications such as Slack or MS Messenger were supposed to reduce email overload. But the result is just an additional overflow. And the flood of emails has not abated at all, on the contrary. Work is most frequently interrupted by emails, on average 3.3 times per hour. It is only in companies where chat services or project management applications are used for internal communication that email has been relegated to second place as a source of disruption.[3]

What has changed is the nature of the disruption. According to the Microsoft Trend Index, between February 2020 and February 2021, the amount of time we spend online in Microsoft Teams meetings more than doubled globally (2.5x).[4] This has led to a lot of people turning off the camera during meetings and trying to do their work at the same time. But this multitasking slows us down, makes us unproductive, produces mediocre results and, most importantly, creates stress.

Productivity drops at an above-average rate because work processes are constantly interrupted by emails. Employees are increasingly suffering from "email stress"—they are tired, frustrated and more irritable.

4.2 Technostress

The study "Healthy digital work?!" looked at digital stress in Germany. The study involved an online survey of 5005 employees who mainly process digital information in a professional context. The researchers concluded that, on average, one in eight respondents is strongly or very strongly affected by stress factors during digital activities. It is striking that this kind of stress tends to be observed more frequently in large companies.[5]

---

[3] E.g. ibid.
[4] Microsoft Corporation. The next great disruption is hybrid work: are we ready? 2021. Available at: https://www.microsoft.com/en-us/worklab/work-trend-index/hybrid-work.
[5] Gimpel, H., Lanzl, J., Regal, C., Urbach, N., Wischniewski S., Tegtmeier, P., Kreilos, M., Kühlmann, T., Becker, J., Eimecke, J., Derra, N. D. Gesund digital arbeiten?! Eine Studie zu digitalem Stress in Deutschland. Augsburg: Projektgruppe Wirtschaftsinformatik des Fraunhofer FIT. 2019. https://doi.org/10.24406/fit-n-562039.

4.2.1 Simultaneity and Diversity Are a Serious Problem

Respondents of this study who work with many different media and technologies but tend to use them rather infrequently are more affected by stressors than those who work with few media and technologies but use them frequently. Digital stress was found to be associated with poorer general health in the survey. In addition, Gimpel and colleagues conclude that digital stress increases fatigue and cognitive and emotional irritation. Digital stress can also lead to lower job satisfaction and productivity. In extreme cases, digital stress can lead to a change of position or career for the affected employees.[6]

4.2.2 Technostress as a Clinical Picture

In a survey of 444 Facebook users, researchers examined the relationship between technostress and technology addiction in relation to social media use. The use of information technology can trigger stress in those affected.[7]

This form of stress is called technostress. The use of social media is related to the perception of stress. People affected by stress react to stressful situations with different coping behaviours. These are aimed at avoiding the stressful situation. In the case of stress caused by one's own activities in social media, a common coping strategy is to reduce or even stop one's own use.

4.2.3 Surprising Research

However, there are studies where people continue to use social media even when they feel stressed. People were observed who, while being stressed, tried to keep up with social media and responded to news.

---

[6] Ibid.
[7] Tarafdar, M., Maier, C., Laumer, S., & Weitzel, T. Explaining the link between technostress and technology addiction for social networking sites: A study of distraction as a coping behavior. Information Systems Journal. 2020;30(1):96–124.

Despite the stressful situation, users found it difficult to turn off social media. These research results show that people who are stressed by social media can become addicted to it.[8]

The contradiction that stress is related to addiction in social media consumption poses new challenges for research.

4.3 Smartphones Waste our Brain Power

Thanks to the smartphone, almost everyone is accessible everywhere—the Internet is a constant companion, providing information, news and conversations with friends. That is why we use our mobile phones so much and take them with us wherever we go, whether it is a restaurant, a café or the beach.

This constant availability has a downside: it reduces our cognitive performance, meaning, the overall functioning and effectiveness of our brain. For example, our attention and concentration are reduced, we remember less, learn more slowly or are simply less creative. At least that is what researchers at the University of Texas found in a study of 800 people.[9]

4.3.1 Three Groups Examined

In two experiments, the researchers of this study tested how the location of the smartphone affects the brain's performance. For this, they divided the 800 test subjects into three groups: Participants in the first team placed their smartphones on the table, group two carried them in their pockets, and the third group stored the devices in another room.

---

[8] Tarafdar, M., Maier, C., Laumer, S., & Weitzel, T. Explaining the link between technostress and technology addiction for social networking sites: A study of distraction as a coping behavior. Information Systems Journal. 2020;30(1):96–124.
[9] Ward, A. F., Duke, K., Gneezy, A., Bos, M. W. Brain drain: The mere presence of one's own smartphone reduces available cognitive capacity. Journal of the Association for Consumer Research. 2017;2(2):140–154. https://doi.org/10.1086/691462.

Afterwards, all participants completed a test with which the scientists tested the cognitive abilities of the test subjects.[10]

4.3.2 Surprising Result

The result: those who had their smartphone in the other room performed significantly better than the other two groups. According to the researchers, it did not matter whether the smartphone was switched on or off or whether it was lying on the table with the screen facing up or down.[11]

4.3.3 Brain Power Is Wasted

A person's ability to concentrate is apparently already reduced when a smartphone is within sight or reach. The reason: according to the researchers of this study, the brain is actively occupied with not being distracted by the smartphone and wastes part of the available cognitive power on this alone.[12]

So, if you want to engage your brain with more interesting things, you should take a break from your smartphone and store your favourite in another room.

4.4 What Does this Mean for Leadership?

4.4.1 For Managers

Efficiency killers are serious issues that we constantly face as modern people. Very often these aspects of concentration and performance deficits are blamed on the more open and flexible office structures because it is easier to blame them.

---

[10] Ibid.
[11] Ward, A. F., Duke, K., Gneezy, A., Bos, M. W. Brain drain: The mere presence of one's own smartphone reduces available cognitive capacity. Journal of the Association for Consumer Research. 2017;2(2):140–154. https://doi.org/10.1086/691462.
[12] Ibid.

As a manager, it is particularly important to be aware of these efficiency killers because you have a dual role. On the one hand as a user, which you are yourself, and on the other hand as a manager. It is important to ask yourself how you use these efficiency killers, how you deal with these issues, and to become aware of how much we have already automated to such an extent that we no longer perceive the stress as such, because the addictive behaviour is greater. This is now also a challenge for research and psychology.

Only when you have dealt with the issue yourself is it possible to start making small changes to your behaviour. By consciously turning off automatic email notifications or consciously checking your email only three times a working day. That you have the "strength" to move those precious mobile phones into another room and, if you want to go one step further, switch them off completely. That you do not have to share everything with everyone all the time on social media—in business or in your private life. You do not have to take a picture of every meal and post it, and you do not have to reply to or like every post.

All these things sound so banal and simple, and yet they are so difficult to do if they are to be more than just a good New Year's resolution. Keeping at it and being constantly aware of what you are doing and how you are doing it. It is quite difficult and hard work.

4.4.2 For Employees

As a superior, you have a different responsibility regarding efficiency killers, which you can only perceive authentically if you constantly reflect on yourself. That is actually the most difficult thing about it all. In my consulting work, I have often found that it is difficult enough for managers to reflect on themselves, which often fails to happen due to the high workload. So how can you authentically reflect on your staff?

It can only be done by consciously taking yourself out of the situation and investing time mentally and emotionally. It is almost impossible to perceive others or even yourself when you are stressed. It spirals down even further because you keep trying unsuccessfully and can only fail.

But what *can* you do?

A first step is to actively address these aspects of concentration and performance problems in team meetings. Here you will probably already be met with astonishment because this is not usual either. In today's working society, we do not like to talk about negative issues or deal with critical feedback. That makes it even more difficult because you also need to find the balance between giving feedback and making something positive happen.

But it is also important to discuss and look for solutions together as a team to identify and partially close performance gaps. This does not replace an individual performance meeting. This discussion with the whole team has a different focus. It is important that a certain level of trust is established in the team so that people have the courage to talk about it.

As a manager, it would also be extremely helpful to keep an eye on one's own employees and to recognise in time when stress reactions become noticeable. But again, it is clear to me that this is not only a sensitive process that also needs courage from the manager but is also based on a strong self-awareness.

An open office structure can be supportive here because it allows for more transparency. However, it is important to recognise the signs correctly and to walk through the office with open ears and eyes. Management by walking and listening to the cues around you.

5
Conflicts in New Working Environments

5.1 It Is Not Immediately a Conflict

Not every dispute is a conflict. The term conflict is derived from the Latin *confligere*, which means to collide, to clash. A conflict is characterised by the fact that:

- Those involved have something to do with each other and are usually dependent on each other in some way.
- There are incongruities in the interests, wishes, concerns of those involved.
- Emotional impairment is experienced by at least one person involved.
- A distinction is made between the factual level and the relationship level of a conflict. The factual level is about numbers, data, facts. The relationship level is about emotions, needs, wishes, self-esteem, attitudes and values.

Conflict arises when there is a difference between a wish, an expectation, a claim and the experienced reality. This difference is usually accompanied by a violation of self-esteem. However, these are often not addressed or are often even considered taboo. This makes conflicts more likely and their resolution more difficult.

5.2 Types of Conflict

Not every interpersonal tension is immediately a conflict and requires intensive confrontation. It is therefore important to recognise teasing, harmless differences of opinion and other moderate tensions between people as such, and not to classify them as conflicts straight away. This is because they are—more often than conflicts—characterised by a lower emotional involvement, a tendency to escalate and a lower influence on the relationship between the persons and thus result in other needs for action.

However, if the situation assumes the proportions of a conflict, it is important to identify it correctly. This means that some kind of diagnosis and reflection must first take place. Distinguishing between the different types of conflict is often quite difficult in practice. Especially when you consider all the other types of conflict. These make it clear that conflicts can have very different causes. Table 5.1 already indicates some approaches to solving the different types of conflict.

Depending on the type of conflict, very different approaches are needed.

Therefore, it is essential to first identify whether there actually is a conflict and, if so, what type of conflict it is.

Figure 5.1 illustrates the different types of conflict at a glance.

5.3 Conflict Phenomena

Conflict situations do something to us. In conflict situations we find it difficult to be rational and in control. When people are in conflict, various "phenomena" occur which ultimately tend to make it more difficult to resolve the conflict (Table 5.2). Being aware of these phenomena and checking yourself to see if you are succumbing to them is an important first step towards conflict resolution.

5 Conflicts in New Working Environments

Table 5.1 Further types of conflict and corresponding approaches to resolving them (adapted from Evangelischer Fachverband für Arbeit und soziale Integration (EFAS))[a]

[a]Type of conflict	Description	Solution approach
Distribution conflict	Unfairly perceived distribution of resources. Feeling of disadvantage, lack of recognition and appreciation.	Address emotional injuries and create "compensations".
Conflict of objectives	Two parties pursue opposing goals. For example, due to different roles or requirements.	Make the goals and needs of the conflict parties transparent.
Conflict of judgement	The goal is clear, but the way to the goal, the procedure to achieve the goal is disputed.	Extensive and differentiated exchange of observations and perceptions.
Relationship conflict	Tensions due to antipathies and personal dislikes. Causes can be values and personality structures or experiences.	Willingness and ability to self-reflect is crucial.
Role conflict	Different expectations due to the function of a person, which is experienced as an inner conflict.	Make different demands conscious and set priorities.

[a]Evangelischer Fachverband für Arbeit und soziale Integration (EFAS) (Ed.). Handout Grundlagen Konfliktbearbeitung & Konfliktmanagement. Available at: https://www.efas-web.de/files/teges/Teges_Handout_Konflikt_FINAL_SCREEN.pdf

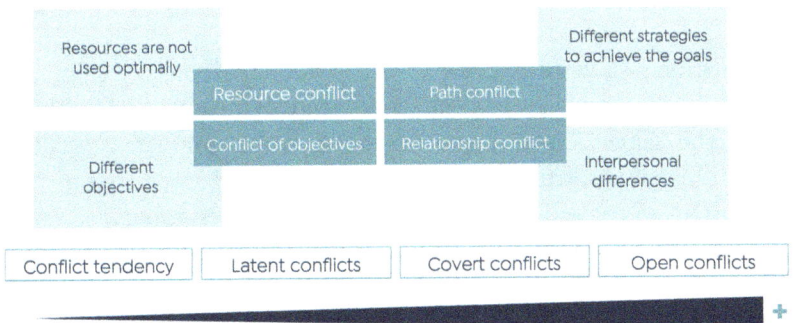

Fig. 5.1 Different types of conflict (Gauer Consulting)

Table 5.2 Central conflict phenomena and their characterisation (adapted from Evangelischer Fachverband für Arbeit und soziale Integration (EFAS))

[a]Conflict phenomenon	Description
Emotional involvement	What is happening occupies you more and more, you cannot let go of it. You revolve around the conflict. Feelings around conflicts are strong, constant and recurring.
Relationship	Unlike an argument, conflicts lead to a "crack" on the relationship level. It is believed that the damage can never be repaired. Impartiality is unthinkable.
Perception	The "colour regulator" is turned away and there is only black and white. We look at everything only through this spotlight. Brooding leads to reinterpretations of behaviour.
Intentions & goals	There must be a winner and a loser of the conflict. Means and goals are linked. When the winner is determined, it is believed, the conflict is resolved.
Behaviour	The participants go out of their way, avoid each other. Sometimes there is also very targeted action and omission (such as withholding information).
Objectivity	A forest of arguments usually camouflages intentions, desires and emotions. The only way to get to the real causes of conflict is to go through the forest.

[a]Evangelischer Fachverband für Arbeit und soziale Integration (EFAS) (Ed.). Handout Grundlagen Konfliktbearbeitung & Konfliktmanagement. Available at: https://www.efas-web.de/files/teges/Teges_Handout_Konflikt_FINAL_SCREEN.pdf

5.4 There Is Potential for Conflict Everywhere

The question is how to respond to this potential. There is potential for conflict in all areas that arise in the context of new working environments. The danger, especially for managers, is that conflicts can take on various dimensions, from hidden signs to open escalation. That is why it is important to recognise more than just signs in good time.

To do this, you need an overview of the potential for conflict in the context of workplace change initiatives. This is particularly useful as a manager.

I have tried to summarise these different issues in a figure (Fig. 5.2). And here the complexity already becomes clear. As a manager, it is

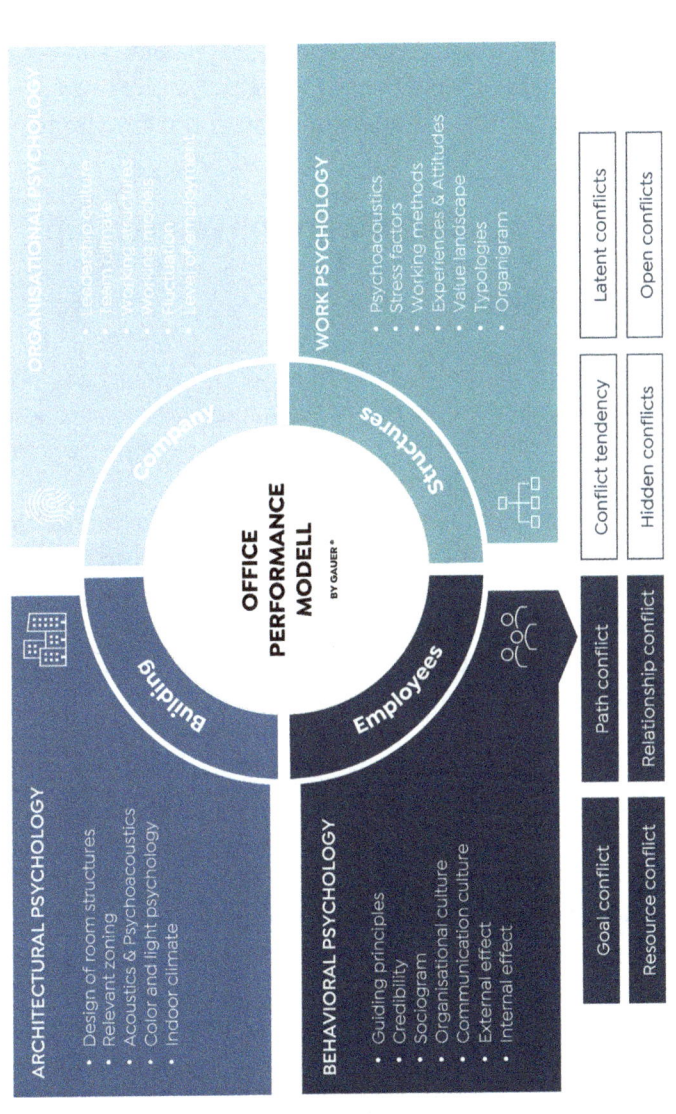

Fig. 5.2 Conflict management model. Conflict potential in new working environments and workplace change initiatives (Gauer Consulting)

important to keep your eyes and ears open to the team and the company in order to recognise conflict tendencies in time.

But it is also important to address these issues with experts as early as the strategy and planning phase, so that the potential for conflict is reduced right from the start of the process. This is easier to do if you have experience of conflict when introducing new working environments.

5.5 What Does this Mean for Leadership?

5.5.1 For Managers

As I mentioned in the previous sections, the problem here in conflict management is again the dual role of the manager. A new working environment is a very emotional issue, even if you try to convince yourself ten times that it is just a relocation.

This means that as a manager, you have to protect yourself first and foremost and deal with the upcoming change yourself in order to avoid any potential for conflict. This is often not done enough, because managers often slide into the change initiative, partly because they have not dealt with it enough themselves, but also—and this is something I often see—because the project initiators and project teams are not sufficiently aware of the scope and complexity of such initiatives. As the focus is usually on the construction/renovation, the layouts and the design, the human components are given too little or no consideration. And this leads to conflicts that build up, usually simultaneously, in different areas (see diagram).

Unfortunately, it is often the case that many workplace initiatives become more and more operationally hectic as time goes on and pressures increase.

As a manager, it is important to be aware of the conflict dimension and not only to link the issues, but also to act with foresight. This is a challenging task on top of day-to-day business.

The first step is to become aware of and sensitive to these cross-cutting issues and their triggers. Rome was not built in a day, and the same is true of new working environments; anything else would be a fallacy.

5.5.2 For Employees

For employees, change often means uncertainty and stress. This is why they look for stability and direction. As a manager, it is extremely important to be aware of these sensitivities. This does not mean that you need to hold hands with every employee, but that you keep your eyes and ears open to see what reactions, attitudes and statements are present.

Furthermore, it is important to communicate properly and to take people along on the journey. This is difficult, especially in the day-to-day business, but it is an investment in the future that will pay off time and again. Employees need their superiors, even if today we increasingly assume that hierarchies must be flat and that because everyone is self-managed and confident, they do not need support.

From my many years of experience, I can say that managers are the big lever for employees and have an incredibly responsible task. It is enormously important to strengthen managers so that they can support their employees in the way that the complexity of new working environments demands.

6

The Human in the Field of Tension Between the Real and the Virtual World

6.1 Cool Environments, Styled Layouts, Happy Office

If it were that easy to make working environments and leadership styles an efficiency booster through heavily designed layouts in cool office structures, and at the same time make everyone happy, then we would have hit the jackpot.

But somehow it is the other way round—what happened? In recent years, illnesses such as burnout, exhaustion and depression have increased significantly. Digitalisation has progressed at an enormous speed. The demand for flexibility in terms of space and people has multiplied, and hybrid working has become a permanent feature. Everything has developed at breakneck speed. But the level of performance has not increased exponentially. This raises the question: what has an influence on our level of performance and well-being?

6.2 Work Routes Must Be Used Efficiently

People are spending more and more time commuting to work. This is not only a national phenomenon, but a global one. Cities such as Mexico City, London, Berlin, Paris, Singapore, Sydney and Toronto are among those with the most extreme commuting conditions in the world.[1]

Increasing traffic congestion is contributing to the need for a fundamental change in the office to make the long commute worthwhile again.

Rapid economic growth—with many new jobs created in big cities without enough affordable housing—is pushing people out of city centres. Remote work is not always a solution, even if some jobs and tasks lend themselves to it.

Harvard Business Review recently reported on a 4-year study by a large technology company that found that communication with employees who work outside the office decreases by as much as 80 per cent compared to team members who are physically located in a shared work environment.[2] It is also important to remember that not every job can be done outside the office. According to Steelcase, 23 per cent of companies expect to continue using the office as their main workplace in the future (Fig. 6.1). The majority of companies (72 per cent) are moving towards a hybrid working model.[3]

6.2.1 Collaboration Is Changing

As employees have to travel longer distances, it is of great importance that the actual work after arriving at the office runs smoothly and productively and is invigorating.

---

[1] Inrix. Inrix 2022. Global Traffic Scorecard. INRIX Global Traffic Rankings. 2023, March 14. Available at: Inrix. https://inrix.com/scorecard/#city-ranking-list.
[2] Bernstein, E. & Waber, B. The truth about open offices. Harvard Business Review. 2021, September 2. Available at: https://hbr.org/2019/11/the-truth-about-open-offices.
[3] Steelcase. Changing Expectations and the Future of Work – Insights from the pandemic to create a better work experience. (2021). Available at: https://www.steelcase.com/content/uploads/2021/02/2021_AM_SC_Global-Report_Changing-Expectations-and-the-Future-of-Work-2.pdf.

6 The Human in the Field of Tension Between the Real...

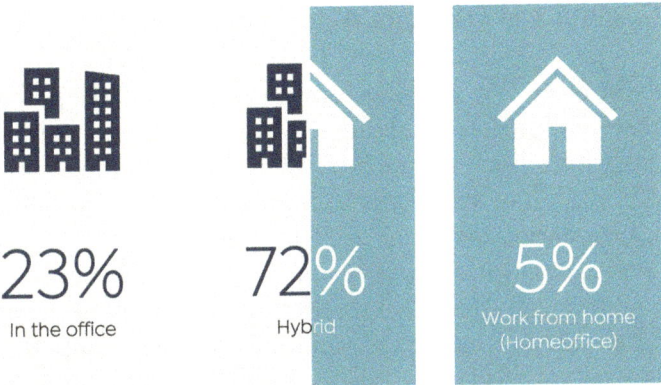

Fig. 6.1 Expectations of companies regarding their future workplace based on the mentioned findings from Steelcase (Gauer Consulting)

Employees are spending more and more time on collaborative work, meaning, working in teams. Companies with a focus on growth rely on collaboration to develop and market innovative ideas. Such high-performing teams work in a new, innovative way. They continuously pass projects from team member to team member, much like a basketball game. Only through joint efforts can they successfully complete a project.

Modern collaboration takes many forms, from continuous teams working together to formal meetings, active brainstorming sessions, informal meetings and spontaneous interactions. The physical presence of all team members enables them to deal with problems immediately in real time, which can be very conducive to a smooth flow of work.

Teams today use a wide variety of methods to make their collaboration efficient and purposeful. Design thinking (creative problem solving) and agile working (rapid implementation) are two such methods—both approaches are characterised by their dynamism and efficiency.

This type of cooperation and the dynamics of such modern teams is in clear contrast to earlier methods, where an employee first completed part of the project and then passed on his or her results to colleagues—similar to a relay race.

6.2.2 Why the Office Is Also Changing

Due to the changes in working practices described in the previous chapter, the workplace is also currently undergoing a transformation. Classic office structures (rows of individual desks, private offices, classic open-plan offices) do not sufficiently support iterative, fast-moving teams or casual, spontaneous meetings.

As a result, companies are investing more space and resources in creating team areas and communal spaces that enable successful and productive teamwork. It is all about multifunctional and zoned office space design—the so-called multi-space office that fully meets the various aspects of flexibility and agility.

What is important, and this is both an opportunity and a risk, is that these multifunctional offices are also designed with employees and the businesses in mind.

6.2.3 Architecture and the Impact on Occupational Psychology

Scientific studies have shown that satisfaction can be influenced by architecture.[4] So far so good—but it is primarily the right to have a say in the design of the workplace that has a positive effect, while fixed guidelines have a negative impact on satisfaction.

The more flexibility is offered in the choice between a fixed workplace and mobile working options (different zones, hybrid working, working from home, etc.), the higher the level of satisfaction. This can also have a positive impact on motivation and performance. However, it is important to find a balance between employees' needs and the company's possibilities. A "positive balance" is needed on both sides in order to be implemented profitably and sustainably.

And this is exactly where we come in.

---

[4] R. Metaj. Architekturpsychologie, Einfluss auf die Arbeit im Büro, Lehrbuchverlag. 2019.

6.2.4 The Office Performance Model

With the Office Performance Model (OPM) (Fig. 6.2), Gauer Consulting has developed a tool that takes these considerations into account and remains part of the process from strategy through planning to implementation. The decision-making and planning chain is always fully comprehensible.

When it comes to workplace transformation, it is crucial to think in cross-disciplinary terms and to harmonise spatial structures with team and organisational structures. Teams need working environments that are not only tailored to their needs but can also be adapted quickly and efficiently without enormous financial or constructional effort.

This requires a more work- and architectural-psychological approach that sees the space as a pedagogical supporter, not as the sole means of efficiency.

Fig. 6.2 The Office Performance Model (OPM). This model is the foundation for the strategic orientation, planning, implementation and utilisation of workplace change projects (Gauer Consulting)

7

The Power of the Built Environment on our Experience and Behaviour

7.1 Architectural-Psychological Perspectives

The application of psychological principles in architecture is an effective and efficient method to raise modern working environments to a new level. With the knowledge of psychology, we can not only design spaces, but also influence the human psyche. Through the skilful design of spaces, latently existing conflicts can be improved. The human being as a key element for high performance requires a harmonious interaction of intellect, culture and architectural psychology. It can be compared to lubricating oil or sand in a gearbox, the former promoting performance while the latter diminishes it.

On the one hand, a person is an active creator of their environment, but on the other hand, they are also a passive user. Thus, a reciprocal relationship results. Built environments can affect people in three different ways.

The direct biological effect is usually unconscious. Colour psychology, for example, plays an important role here, as does the classic indoor environment, such as temperature, humidity or air quality.

The conscious, psychological effect is the most visible and is directly related to the way we evaluate spaces in our context. Well-being results from a positive evaluation of space, while dissatisfaction results from a negative evaluation of space. The semi-conscious and also the unconscious psychological effect has to do with the patterns of movement in the space as well as the cooperation of people in these spaces and the available space.

As early as the 1960s, Lévi-Strauss observed that people can be changed in their attitudes by changing their foundations and patterns. An interesting example of this is the Bororo tribe in South America, who originally followed a nature religion. This belief system contained important rules for their social coexistence. Missionaries tried to convert the tribe to Christianity. But they quickly realised that the surest way to "convert" the tribe was to change their village structure. They arranged the houses according to the European row house principle, which differed considerably from the communal and cross-hierarchical character of the Bororo tribe (Fig. 7.1).[1]

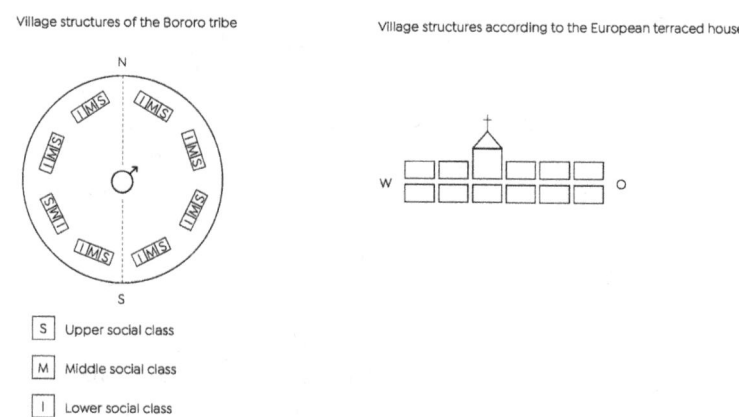

Fig. 7.1 Simplified schematic representation of the cross-hierarchical village structure of the Bororo tribe in South America (left figure) and the structure introduced by missionaries according to the European row house principle (right figure) (Gauer Consulting)

---

[1] Lévi-Strauss, C. Strukturale Anthropologie. Frankfurt/M.: Suhrkamp, 1967.

And lo and behold… they had laid the groundwork for a new system.

As sad as this observation is, it clearly shows how spatial structures can affect our way of being together.

7.2 Recognising Connections

There is a close connection between our state of exhaustion and our energy level. The spectrum ranges from moments in which we cannot concentrate and have to start our thoughts all over again, to phases in which we are in flow and our ideas follow one another effortlessly. The people around us also play a role: whether they disturb us by once again having something to discuss in the vicinity of our workspace, or whether we actively and interestedly engage in the conversation as well.

The interaction between the space we are in and our own mood and self-perception is of crucial importance. These factors have a significant influence on our perception of the surrounding conditions and can either support or impair our well-being (Fig. 7.2).

Fig. 7.2 Mental and physical well-being in physical space. Architectural and individual factors affect the perception of environmental conditions and influence psychological and physical well-being both through this mediator and directly (Gauer Consulting)

7.3 Maslow's Experiment

An experiment by A. Maslow, which was conducted as early as the 1950s, describes this interaction between feeling and space very impressively. The setting: The first room was called "The beautiful room", had large windows, a bookcase, bright light, a very comfortable armchair and a nice carpet. The second room was called "The ugly room", had grey walls, was not very tidy, had a broken lamp and worn furniture. The subjects' task was to sort a stack of portraits (the same portraits for both groups) according to their energy and well-being.[2]

The result was disarmingly clear. The portraits in the beautiful room were perceived much more positively. Even the mood of the experimenters was friendlier, more helpful and more open in the beautiful room, although the experimenters knew about it.[3]

7.4 We Can Contribute

We can strongly influence how we feel and experience things by changing our environment and actively contribute to our happiness and well-being. This is especially important if you are in a leadership position.

Through careful architectural psychology planning in advance of a work environment redesign project and through practical experience in everyday life, we can significantly influence how we feel about the spaces around us.

However, it is important to note that spaces alone are not the solution to all challenges, although they can have a significant impact on us. There are two other crucial factors that strongly influence our perception and experience. On the one hand, there are individual factors such as personal attitudes, values, stress, sleep, worries, fears, etc., and on the other hand, company-related factors such as company culture, cooperation,

---

[2] Maslow, A. H., & Mintz, N. L. Effects of Esthetic Surroundings: I. Initial Effects of Three Esthetic Conditions Upon Perceiving "Energy" and "Well-Being" in Faces, The Journal of Psychology. 1956;41(2): 247–254. DOI: https://doi.org/10.1080/00223980.1956.9713000.

[3] Ibid.

leadership and responsibility play an important role. It is crucial to develop a holistic perspective if you want to design and experience long-term, value-adding and authentic working environments.

7.5 Art Nouveau and New Working Worlds

Art nouveau emerged in the second half of the nineteenth century and reached its peak around the turn of the century (1890–1910). It developed in Europe as a reaction to industrialisation and the effects of technological progress on art and society (counter-movement).

Art nouveau artists sought to integrate nature into the modern world, making art and aesthetics more tangible for everyone. Motifs inspired by nature, such as sweeping lines and shapes, tendrils and waves, are considered central features of art nouveau.

Art nouveau influenced painting, sculpture, architecture and furniture design, as well as the production of jewellery and glassware.

The bourgeoisie played a key role in promoting and disseminating art nouveau. The emerging middle class had access to education and culture during industrialisation and was looking for a new identity and aesthetic forms of expression. Art nouveau offered a way of standing out from traditional styles and expressing one's own social advancement and cultural taste. The bourgeoisie supported artists financially by buying art, furniture and decorative objects in the art nouveau style.

Although art nouveau is often associated with the bourgeoisie, it also appealed to workers and craftsmen. The idea of a unity of art and craft resonated well with the ideology of the labour movement, which emphasised manual labour and human creativity over machine mass production. In some cases, art nouveau was present in working-class communities and was seen as a means of improving the quality of life and working environment.

The upper class, which included wealthy aristocrats and entrepreneurs, also contributed to the development of art nouveau. Some artists and designers had privileged access to this class and received commissions for opulent, high-quality works of art and interiors. The upper classes valued the innovation and originality of art nouveau and often used it as an expression of status and wealth.

What does this mean for new working environments?

As mentioned above, art nouveau had a lasting influence on architecture and furniture design and was created in an era very similar to the one we are experiencing now. This means that we are not at the beginning of these ideas, but that the complexity and interdependencies have already been experienced. We do not have to reinvent the wheel, we can combine the experience of the past with the present and use it to shape a sustainable future!

This is incredibly exciting, and the possibilities are vast and can help us to redefine ourselves.

Like the new world of work, art nouveau was not a uniform movement, but had different manifestations in different countries and regions. In the world of work, it is the different companies, cultures and ways of working.

The diversity of social backgrounds of those who influenced art nouveau contributed to the richness and complexity of this aesthetic. It is the same with new working environments, they offer the chance to enrich working life enormously with their diversity.

The art nouveau movement united people from different social backgrounds in their efforts to establish a new artistic and creative direction that reflected the challenges and opportunities of their time.

With workplace initiatives, we unite people from different backgrounds, teams, working models, personalities, etc. and create a new type of working environment that reflects the challenges of our time and helps us to work efficiently, well and healthily.

8

The Virtual Space

8.1 Out of the Office or in the Office?

Working from home is one of those matters: One man's joy is another man's sorrow. It is an ongoing topic in many companies and is constantly being discussed anew. From my many years of consulting experience, I have to say that the implementation of home office options has to be handled sensitively. It depends very much on the respective company, the personality, as well as the private situation of the employees, the activity and the area of responsibility. In other words, a whole series of interdependencies that influence each other.

In the meantime, there are already a number of studies that deal scientifically with this topic. I will present a few of them to you in the following. Nevertheless, I would like to state the following. It is very important—and here I refer again to Chap. 2 "The Art of Introspection"—to find a mixture that suits the people involved and this can be very different. For me, the question is not so much how much working from home or "in office", but rather what do we need as a team in order to work together efficiently, authentically, in a value-creating and healthy way? And here again, managers are very much in demand. To find the individual mix that allows for manageable diversity.

So, now to the promised studies.

A study conducted by the University of Konstanz in October 2022 revealed the following findings. The desire for working from home and mobile working remained constant throughout the study at an average of 2.9 days per week. There is also a strong desire for hybrid working—64 per cent of respondents said in April 2022 that they wanted a work situation where they could work flexibly from both home and the office. Only 10 per cent prefer to work exclusively in the office and 26 per cent would like to work from home full time. These findings support the current trend towards hybrid working. Employees clearly want individual flexibility in their choice of work location.[1]

The 2022 KOFA study (Competence Centre for Securing Skilled Labour) also shows that companies expect more than a quarter of employees to be using the option of mobile working or working from home in 2022. Both managers and employees without personnel responsibility will be able to work on a mobile basis to a greater extent than in 2019.[2]

In 2019, only 15.3 per cent of companies said their employees are able to work remotely several days a week; for 2022, 29.5 per cent expect this to be the case. There is also an increase among managers, from 23.4 per cent in 2019 to 34.1 per cent in 2022.[3]

So, as you can see, the desire for hybrid working options is there, it has even increased, and at the same time we must always ask ourselves how far we can go. At what point is the desire no longer feasible and perhaps also no longer expedient. So—in short—a critical examination is crucial for success.

---

[1] Kunze, F., & Zimmermann, S. Die Transformation zu einer hybriden Arbeitswelt: Ergebnisbericht zur Konstanzer Homeoffice Studie 2020–2022. 2022b. Available at: http://nbn-resolving.de/urn:nbn:de:bsz:352-2-ai5pzcioansj3.

[2] Koneberg, F., Lehr, J., Seyda, S. & Werner, D. Herausforderungen und Chancen hybrider Arbeit (Kompetenzzentrum Fachkräftesicherung (KOFA), Eds.). June, 2022. Available at: https://www.kofa.de/daten-und-fakten/studien/herausforderungen-und-chancen-hybrider-arbeit/.

[3] Koneberg, F., Lehr, J., Seyda, S. & Werner, D. Herausforderungen und Chancen hybrider Arbeit (Kompetenzzentrum Fachkräftesicherung (KOFA), Eds.). June, 2022. Available at: https://www.kofa.de/daten-und-fakten/studien/herausforderungen-und-chancen-hybrider-arbeit/.

8.2 Work Life and Private Life Blur Together

Many of us are confronted with a dilemma here. How do I create a balance between private time and working time? From my own experience, I can say that it is extremely hard to separate the two. I only manage to work from home when the children are at school or still asleep—and even then, I am always surprised at how many things I "have" to do around the house at once. Or what I just remember in between, what still needs to be done urgently.

Due to the increasing flexibility in the world of work, exactly these clear demarcations between different areas of life such as work and private life are becoming blurred. This requires employees working in mobile work models to redefine their personal boundaries between these areas and to question their own needs and behaviour.

Especially for people who work from home, it is of great importance to consciously set boundaries between their work and family commitments, as they perform both professional and family roles in their home. These intermingling spheres of life can favour the emergence of conflicts where, on the one hand, work can intrude into aspects of private and family life, while, on the other hand, private matters can interfere with professional tasks. And here we have another facet of detachment—I will call it a "change of scenery". We humans need variety in our brains in order to work well, efficiently and/or creatively. This promotes concentration and facilitates productive work. When people are in a home office, they often only stay in the vicinity of their flat or house. Of course, this makes it more difficult, even just visually, to set boundaries and the brain gets too few external impulses. This is a super-exciting process that should at least be thought through.

Then there is another facet of demarcation that is actually an important factor for us humans. Namely, the trip to the office! This definitely and justifiably has its mental and emotional advantages. Because in this "travelling time" you have the opportunity to consciously "let go" of issues from the office or to literally drive away from them.

8.3 Team Spirit Decreases but Employer Attractiveness Increases

The hybrid world of work is not that easy to navigate and presents companies with several challenges but, when you find the right mix, also numerous opportunities. In order to analyse these, the KOFA Competence Centre for Securing Skilled Workers examined the influence of hybrid work in an extensive company survey.

Challenges arise particularly in the area of leadership culture: More than half of the companies surveyed (52.3 per cent) report increased demands on managers due to hybrid work models. What does not surprise me at all—it is completely logical—is that leadership is easier in the context of proximity than in the context of distance. The spontaneous exchange is missing, the quick information in the corridor, the short meeting on the topic and maybe even the spontaneous after-work beer together. These are incredibly important elements of working well together. The results confirm my observation and point of view. They show a decline in team spirit (55.2 per cent) and reduced opportunities for knowledge sharing and networking (35.5 per cent) are perceived as adverse effects of hybrid work. And that, if I may say so, is not without danger. Because team spirit is a powerful engine for performance and loyalty.[4]

Furthermore, companies feel that individual work performance is less evident due to hybrid work (35.9 per cent).[5] These statements by the companies are also understandable and comprehensible. It takes a lot of trust and mutual understanding to integrate hybrid working as an active part of everyday work. It is often not that simple—at least not in the long run. People lose closeness to each other. That doesn't have to be a showstopper, but you have to balance it well.

On the other hand, hybrid work also opens up opportunities: almost half of the companies surveyed (48.8 per cent) note an increased

---

[4] Koneberg, F., Lehr, J., Seyda, S. & Werner, D. Herausforderungen und Chancen hybrider Arbeit (Kompetenzzentrum Fachkräftesicherung (KOFA), Eds.). June, 2022. Available at: https://www.kofa.de/daten-und-fakten/studien/herausforderungen-und-chancen-hybrider-arbeit/.
[5] Ibid.

attractiveness for employers. In addition, almost four out of ten companies report increased motivation and satisfaction among their employees (38.1 per cent) as well as increased flexibility within the company (39.5 per cent). Many companies also see improved opportunities for securing skilled workers through hybrid working models (28.6 per cent), for example by recruiting new skilled workers or extending working hours for part-time workers.[6]

However, we must not forget one thing, and here I am definitely a cautionary voice again: these studies refer to a short period of time. We don't really have much experience with these hybrid ways of working. The good thing is that we can always continue to learn, try out and study.

The cautionary part is that we have to remain critical, not make too many concessions for the wrong reasons, but find a consensus that will stand the test of time. But that means for us—and for all leaders among you even more—we have to look together for solutions that are coherent in themselves and with us.

8.4 Loneliness

Now we have another hot topic, the tendency of which is massively increasing. There are more and more people on earth—and yet it is evident that loneliness is increasing enormously worldwide. In Germany, for example, 42 per cent felt lonely in 2021, one of the reasons being the Corona pandemic.[7] Corona is now over, but loneliness has remained and continues to multiply like a new virus.

Another important finding is that it is not only older people who feel lonely. During the Corona pandemic, young people were the most affected by loneliness. Even social media could not compensate for the loss of social contacts. And that is where I bring in my buzz phrase again: people need people, and real people, standing or sitting in front of you!

---

[6] Ibid.
[7] Entringer, T. Epidemiologie von Einsamkeit in Deutschland. Institut für Sozialarbeit und Sozialpädagogik eV Kompetenznetz Einsamkeit. 2022.

In this context, let us look at the example of the mobile worker who, by definition, is regularly cut off from his or her workplace and the social and professional—and above all spontaneous—interactions associated with it. Or if we put it "pro-mobile", having different choices of workplaces, we are confronted with loneliness and isolation as central challenges of mobile working. Whether we want to admit it or not.

Many people in today's working world believe that the much-discussed digital networking combined with the slogan "work anywhere and whenever you want" really suits human nature. This is also reflected in terms like "workation", a mix between "work" and "vacation", which describes the active linking of work and holiday. In practice, workation means moving the workplace to an attractive location or a cool holiday destination. This concept is now heavily promoted and celebrated as part of New Work.

Nevertheless, this concept should be taken with a grain of salt. Because what sounds cool for the first time can often be associated with a lot of stress. I myself have been working this way for years, even long before there were fancy terms for it. From my own experience, I can say that it requires enormous discipline not to be constantly glued in front of the laptop. When I was asked after the last autumn holidays how it was on the Côte d'Azur, my answer was: the surroundings were nice, the terrace too … But at the end of the day, I often felt guilty because I had not spent enough time with my family. Sometimes I close the laptop and feel lonely, even though I had video calls with different people throughout the day. But in reality, I was neither with these real people nor with my real family.

8.5 Trust Among Colleagues

We are fundamentally struggling with the basic value of trust—giving trust, having trust, this has a lot to do with our global political problem situation, as well as with our social directions and counter directions.

It would be naïve to believe that this problem does not extend into working life. But what also comes into play here is that trust is a very fragile thing. It takes a long time to build it up, but it can be destroyed or greatly reduced again relatively quickly. On the one hand, this has to do with how people deal with each other, which is of course a challenge in itself in modern, open office structures. On the other hand, it also has to do with whether you see each other or not, or whether you see each other in real or virtual terms.

The relationship between colleagues is a delicate bond that develops over time. During times of change, as we have been experiencing for a few years, from very analogue to extremely digital, not only is the sensitivity of this relationship heightened, but also its fragility. Suddenly, even the smallest differences can lead to decisive changes.

There are now well-founded results from various studies that show what consequences too much "personal distance" can have on the relationship between colleagues and their basis of trust.

In June 2021, the University of Konstanz conducted a survey to find out whether the pandemic and the associated working practices had a negative impact on the respondents' emotional attachment to their colleagues. When evaluating the results, the respondents were divided into three groups:

(1) primarily office based (less than 33 per cent of work is mobile).
(2) hybrid work (between 34–65 per cent is mobile work),
(3) predominantly mobile work (more than 66 per cent of work is mobile).

Overall, 27 per cent of all participants said that they felt a lower emotional connection to their colleagues since the beginning of the pandemic. This perception strongly depended on the work model in which the person in question worked—whether they worked predominantly on-site in the office, in hybrid structures or in a home office.[8]

In detail, it showed that only 21 per cent of the employees who worked mainly in the office felt a reduced emotional bond with their colleagues. In the hybrid work models, it was 29 per cent of respondents who reported decreasing emotional attachment. Among those who worked

---

[8] Kunze, F., & Zimmermann, S. Die Transformation zu einer hybriden Arbeitswelt: Ergebnisbericht zur Konstanzer Homeoffice Studie 2020–2022. 2022b. Available at: http://nbn-resolving.de/urn:nbn:de:bsz:352-2-ai5pzcioansj3.

mainly from home in the home office, as many as 33 per cent reported that their emotional attachment to colleagues had diminished.[9]

So, it seems that trust and emotional connection within teams and organisations is becoming a challenge that organisations and their leaders need to address, particularly with hybrid workers and those who are predominantly mobile.[10]

Another very exciting study from the Massachusetts Institute of Technology in 2022, which not only examined pandemic-related changes in people's sense of connectedness and loneliness, came to very similar conclusions.[11]

This presents us with great challenges, because we are dealing with a very deep-seated emotion that cannot be turned off and on at the "push of a button".

It is clear and unambiguous that the desire for hybrid work remains among employees and that the pandemic has also revolutionised employers' attitudes towards flexible working arrangements. Many employees want to continue to reap at least some of the benefits of working from home, but over time the costs of this approach are becoming more apparent.

While employees appreciate the time savings, the elimination of commuting stress and the flexibility to better balance work and personal demands, there are unmistakable disadvantages to working from home that go beyond domestic distractions and blurred boundaries between work and personal life.

In particular, the quality, frequency and nature of interactions have been shown to change when colleagues are physically separated, and there is less dynamic, spontaneous communication.[12]

Let us now turn to brain research on this topic. Neuroscience research has shown that only face-to-face encounters trigger the full range of physiological responses and neural synchronisation required for optimal

---

[9] Ibid.
[10] Ibid.
[11] Knight, C., Olaru, D., Lee, J., & Parker, S. The loneliness of the hybrid worker. MIT Sloan Management Review. 2022.
[12] Knight, C., Olaru, D., Lee, J., & Parker, S. The loneliness of the hybrid worker. MIT Sloan Management Review. 2022.

human communication and trust building. Furthermore, digital channels such as video conferencing have been found to interfere with our processing of communicative information. Such limited virtual interactions can lead to static and closed-off collaboration networks, workers with a diminished sense of belonging to their organisation, and social and professional isolation.[13]

8.6 Trust in Superiors

But what about trust in superiors? Of course, this is also a topic that should not be underestimated, especially in modern, open working environments. I recently read an article about the importance of "high trust companies". And what surprised me was that mistrust, the opposite of trust, is present on both sides. 38 per cent of managers are sceptical about their remote workers, and now on top of that: half of the employees feel "micromanaged" in general.[14] For me, these are strong interpretative results.

This raises the question of how companies have made the transition to regular remote working and how this has affected trust? The Capgemini Research Institute has produced some interesting results here.

Burnout rates among remote workers are increasing significantly. Over half of employees feel burnt out due to mobile work and home office, and among younger employees aged 31–40, this number rises as high as 61 per cent. Employees express concerns about long-term remote working, which negatively impacts their engagement, satisfaction and also their productivity. 56 per cent fear the stresses and demands of being "online" all the time. Employees also feel that the organisation does not trust them enough and controls them too much. Furthermore, new employees feel

---

[13] E.g. Yang, L., Holtz, D., Jaffe, S. et al. The effects of remote work on collaboration among information workers. Nat Hum Behav, 2022;6:43–54. https://doi.org/10.1038/s41562-021-01196-4.

[14] Lamothe, I., Duruflé, B.T., Kirstein-Bandmierowski, M. (2021, September 3). Trust at the Heart of Hybrid Working. Capgemini. https://www.capgemini.com/insights/expert-perspectives/trust-at-the-heart-of-hybrid-working/.

lost and not involved in a remote environment. Half of them said they would quit if mobile working was the only option.[15]

Further findings from the University of Konstanz show how the relationship of trust with their manager had developed. Here, as many as 10 per cent of respondents have the impression that their manager trusts them less since the start of the pandemic.[16] For me, this is already an indication that distance between people—also in the case of working people—bears problems.

Again, it is interesting to divide the results according to the participants who work mainly in presence, in hybrid or mobile working models. Of the respondents who work mainly in the office, 9 per cent reported that their relationship with their supervisors had deteriorated. Among those who work exclusively mobile, it was 7 per cent, and among those who work mainly hybrid, as many as 14 per cent reported that their relationship of trust with their managers had suffered.[17]

These findings suggest that especially in hybrid work environments, the trust relationship between managers and employees is a challenge that needs to be addressed.

And for me, these clearly show that trust can be promoted or inhibited by important elements and ways of dealing with people.

Element one: Many employees feel controlled by their superiors and have the feeling that they are not given enough freedom. I find this incredibly intriguing, because I have had many other experiences that at least put this statement into perspective. I often experience that employees want to have more responsibility and more freedom, but this is in contrast to their performance. They simply cannot deliver—and that is ultimately very time-consuming for everyone involved. I regularly observe with clients, but also with us in the company, that self-perception does not always correspond to the perception of others. And that of course

---

[15] Crummenerl, C., Paolini, S., Perronet, C., Lamothe, I., Ravindranath, S., Schastok, I., Buvat, J., Manchanda, N., Aggarwal, G., & Chakraborty, A. The future of work: from remote to hybrid. Capgemini Research Institute. Luettavissa: https://www.capgemini.com/fi-en/wp-content/uploads/sites/27/2020/12/Report-The-Future-of-Work.pdf. Luettu, 2, 2020.

[16] Kunze, F., & Zimmermann, S. Die Transformation zu einer hybriden Arbeitswelt: Ergebnisbericht zur Konstanzer Homeoffice Studie 2020–2022. 2022b. Available at: http://nbn-resolving.de/urn:nbn:de:bsz:352-2-ai5pzcioansj3.

[17] Ibid.

makes it relatively difficult to deal with, because we also move in a very inclusive and "woke" society and also need to be aware of how people are reacting to world events and trends at the moment. These are all factors that we cannot completely ignore, because they have a huge impact on how people think about themselves and others.

Element two is clearly the physical proximity, in my opinion. People need people, because in the long run, distance and too much virtual contact is counterproductive in every respect. No matter how much we try to make everything sound better, humans have a herd instinct, which makes extreme sense from an evolutionary-biological point of view. It is a matter of finally understanding this and creating working environments that support this idea. But to do that, we also have to start thinking in a new way.

Element three is basically the supreme discipline. The magic word is authenticity. In order to have a real chance to make a positive difference and, above all, to really reach people, an authentic way of acting and thinking is the be-all and end-all. And I mean it literally: it is the beginning and the end in every situation. We psychologists speak of the so-called "honest signals" that other people perceive and which convey our genuine attitude to the outside world—whether we like it or not! This principle also originates from primeval times and was essential for survival back then. You could simply not spend all your time discussing something and debating the pros and cons. Act or die, flee or attack. And for that we needed quick and honest signals that were far from language. It is no coincidence that an old saying goes: Talk is silver—silence is gold. Sometimes we should talk less and act more, or even just "be".

8.7 What Does this Mean for Leadership?

8.7.1 For Managers

I would recommend taking a closer look at the three elements described above—control, closeness, authenticity—and listening to how you feel about them. Because it is important to deal with the topic yourself and to actively analyse aspects in relation to yourself. As a manager, you are also in a constant field of tension, because you also work hybrid in part, of course.

Managers also have a key role to play here, as they can set things in motion to reduce feelings of loneliness and isolation. But it is not about breaking out into operational hectic and finding quick solutions, but first of all about self-reflection and active listening.

I think it is extremely important for a manager to find his or her own approach to leading in new working environments in a way that benefits everyone in the team (including the manager). To implement this, however, a critical examination is indispensable. Because believe me, you can never please everyone anyway, but only give your authentic best! And if you can do that, then you are one giant step further.

Every journey begins with the first step …

8.7.2 For Employees

Leaders are also particularly needed here so that there is a chance of keeping the fragile structure together and not losing anyone along the way. This can be difficult, because a multitude of "I's" come together. We all talk about the "we", but many people act very much from the "I" perspective. In principle, that is totally okay and it is what makes us who we are.

But this security is only enough until a certain point, because sustainable survival—and here I refer again to evolutionary biology—is only guaranteed if we remain in our community. Although today we no longer need to fear sabre-toothed tigers lurking around every corner, there is another kind of threat, namely loneliness, social isolation, frustration, sadness and similar challenges. Our struggles are basically the same as they were 100'000 years ago, except that today we use different tools and have different consequences, but—one way or another—they go to the heart of the matter.

But now back to active possibilities, which you can start using right now. Because sometimes it is also important to generate a few quick wins.

There are first concrete recommendations for action for employees that can have a supporting effect:

- Consciously organise joint lunches or coffee breaks.
- Build mutual understanding and exchange.
- Make use of co-working spaces.
- Value the contribution of mobile workers and make them feel that their well-being is important and actively offer support.
- Appoint someone responsible who specifically looks after the interests of mobile workers—for example, regularly exchanging information with them, providing them with information or organising socialising and network events.
- Have an open ear.
- Walk through the office with open eyes.
- Having the courage to try things out yourself.

It is of great importance that an open exchange and honest, authentic communication between all team members is promoted in the team. It is important that the aspects of hybrid and mobile working are also critically considered and discussed, and that the team actively deals with what works well and what works less well.

9

The Physical Space

9.1 Leadership and Architecture

"Every new situation demands a new architecture."
   Jean Nouvel (French architect)

Architecture is characterised by its distinctiveness. In contrast to other industries, which strive for characteristics such as repeatability, these concepts have only limited applicability in architecture. The architect has to deal with different factors such as typography, climate and regional resources and find a suitable and unique solution.

Our modern working environments, which are often even architectural masterpieces, are jarring to me and I ask myself whether the planning and implementation really meet the requirements of the company and the needs of the employees. From my personal experience I have to say that uniqueness and an approach "adapted to the situation" are often missing.

Now I notice a certain gap here that a manager alone cannot master. But as a leader you can definitely draw attention to this missing match. Or even better: ask the right questions at the beginning. Because very often it is not consciously forgotten, but simply not present in the mindset and in the action steps.

Yet, scientific studies have shown that the satisfaction of employees can be influenced with the help of architecture.[1] The physical design and layout of spaces also have a significant impact on the interaction between employees. An organisational culture is needed that promotes cohesion, support, good relationships and transparency through processes, structures, cultures and appropriate spaces. These elements are what meet the requirements of a healthy organisational culture and appropriate leadership behaviour.

Another factor that is also part of the corporate culture is the right to have a say in the design of the working environment, which has a positive effect on satisfaction, whereas rigid guidelines can have a negative effect.

In my experience, the satisfaction of employees can be positively influenced if they are offered the possibility to flexibly choose between fixed workplaces and mobile work options. This also helps to increase motivation. It is crucial to find a balance between the needs of the employees and the possibilities of the company. A "win-win situation" on both sides is necessary to ensure effective and sustainable implementation.

9.2 Architectural and Psychological Success Factors

Over the years, our preference for trendy, modern and innovative office design has continued to grow, but at the same time we have become a little blind to our basic human needs. We have neglected our own instincts in favour of aesthetic design experiences, because these are easier to see.

Interestingly, it is not so much the classic office design that makes the decisive difference, but rather the psychological incentives and hygiene factors. In my many years of experience in client projects, I have become clearly aware of this, and in the meantime this insight has also been

---

[1] R. Metaj. Architekturpsychologie, Einfluss auf die Arbeit im Büro, Lehrbuchverlag. 2019.

confirmed by science.[2] The factors described below are necessary in the office environment to enable efficient work and create a pleasant working atmosphere.

9.2.1 Designing Spaces: Work-Related and Architectural Factors

It is clear that people have a preference for sitting near windows and enjoying a good view from there.[3] This need arises from the inner stress management mechanism and is pursued intuitively. Another strong need is for fresh air, which becomes an important matter in modern, energy-efficient buildings (e.g. Minergie buildings) where opening windows is often not possible. Here, human needs are in conflict with efficient building technology.

Bright and friendly working environments are important to people, as they find them stimulating and positively charging.[4] Bright interior design in office environments acts like a boost of vitamin D. At the same time, it is important that workplaces are not too close together to ensure a certain amount of privacy. This can be easily achieved through clever zoning, whereby it is important to consider individual needs as well as the needs of teams.

Zoning has the advantage of visually and acoustically dividing the space and enhancing the overall atmosphere, making the office space more attractive. Ambience plays a significant role in the scale of employee needs. It is not about winning design competitions, but about adapting the working environment to the communication culture and working methods of the teams. Colour design that meets the wishes of employees contributes significantly to well-being and concentration, and aspects of colour psychology should be taken into account.

---

[2] E.g. Maidani, E. A. Comparative study of Herzberg's two-factor theory of job satisfaction among public and private sectors. Public personnel management, 1991;20(4):441–448.

[3] E.g. Chang, C., & Chen, P. Human Response to Window Views and Indoor Plants in the Workplace. HortScience HortSci, 2005;40(5):1354–1359.

[4] E.g. Colenberg, S., Jylhä, T., & Arkesteijn, M. The relationship between interior office space and employee health and well-being–a literature review. Building Research & Information. 2021;49(3):352–366.

What also supports employees, specifically stress reduction and the general indoor climate, are plants in the office space.[5] It is fascinating to observe how pictures of plants or the view from a window make a positive contribution to a pleasant atmosphere. In everyday office life, the motto should be "sit, stand and walk", whereby this depends not only on the furniture, but above all on the people themselves.

9.2.2 Understanding People: Structural and Psychological Factors

In agile working environments, the key focus is on flexibility in thinking and acting. A crucial element in achieving this goal is flexible working hours. My practical experience has shown that relationships with colleagues and superiors are of particular importance to employees. The individual personality plays a decisive role in all forms of work, whether in open space, multi-space or traditional structures.

This is because, in addition to the currently much-discussed "Activity-Based Working" (ABW), "Personality Based Working" also contributes significantly to the efficient use of spaces and the creation of a pleasant working atmosphere. Every room design is shaped by people and their individual personalities, which in turn influences how we work and how we perceive our environment.

9.2.3 People and Architecture: An Interplay

The decisive factor is that the diversity of people's personalities and the culture of the company flow into the workplace design and are considered as a whole (Figs. 9.1, 9.2 and 9.3).

My many years of experience in practice as well as scientific findings show that people need people first and foremost and that the office with

---

[5] E.g. Sanchez, J. A., Ikaga, T., & Sanchez, S. V. Quantitative improvement in workplace performance through biophilic design: A pilot experiment case study. Energy and Buildings. 2018;177:316–328.

9 The Physical Space 91

Fig. 9.1 The connection between people and architecture. It is important that the interplay between the experience and behaviour of people and architecture is taken into account in the design of new working environments (Gauer Consulting)

Fig. 9.2 Effects of employees enjoying working in the office on engagement, productivity, identification with the company culture and change of employer, based on Steelcase's findings mentioned in the text above (Gauer Consulting)

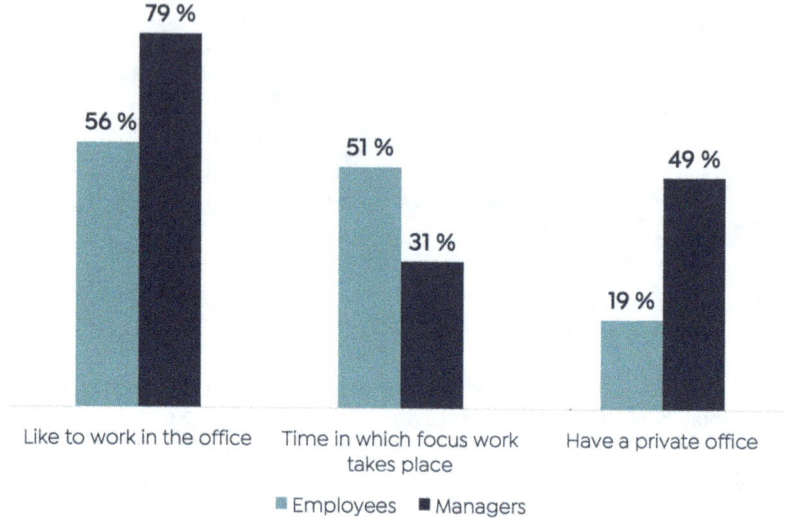

Fig. 9.3 Differences between employees and managers in terms of the availability of a private office in the company, the time they spend on focus work and whether they like working in the office, based on Steelcase's findings mentioned in the text (Gauer Consulting)

the developed workplace design primarily supports them and not the other way around (Fig. 9.1).

9.3 Research Findings

9.3.1 Employees Enjoy Working in the Office

Steelcase researchers conducted a comprehensive study of various factors that significantly influence engagement, productivity, cultural connectedness and propensity to change jobs. They considered current concerns in the business world, such as salary and the possibility of hybrid work models, as well as other factors such as commute time, company affiliation and company size.

Not surprisingly, the findings (Fig. 9.2) show that whether or not employees enjoy working in the office has the greatest impact on employee engagement, productivity and sense of belonging to the organisation. In terms of employee engagement, length of service is the most important factor, followed by how much employees enjoy working on-site at the office. According to Steelcase, employees who enjoy working in the office are 33 per cent more engaged, 30 per cent more likely to identify with the company culture, 9 per cent more productive and 20 per cent less likely to change employers. For a visual representation of these findings, see Fig. 9.2.[6]

These are all wonderful figures that show us that there is the possibility of going "up". That is also the reason why I include these findings here. My point is not so much that we analyse the numbers and try to achieve them, but rather to show that we have effects that we should pay attention to.

Especially at a time when the number of people unable to work is soaring, there is a shortage of skilled workers, people want to work part-time and the baby boomers are retiring. Now is definitely the time to rethink and look at how we can actively incorporate the world of work into our new situation and really use it in a meaningful and sustainable way.

The lessons learned serve to ensure that we do not lose sight of the way forward. It is important to understand that the numbers are different in every company, and rightly so. However, it is crucial that we actively address the issues of architecture and corporate culture in order to have a real chance of successfully implementing innovations.

9.3.2 Managers Prefer Going to the Office to Employees

The vast majority of respondents have a dedicated workspace at home. Those who do not have such a dedicated space are often ordinary employees. However, these regular employees are less likely to have access to their own office in the company than managers (see Fig. 9.3). Nevertheless, they spend more than half of their working time on concentrated work,

---

[6] Steelcase Inc. Das neue Zeitalter der hybriden Arbeit. Was die Angestellten jetzt brauchen – Wie Gemeinschaft am Arbeitsplatz entsteht (Global Report). February, 2022. Available at: https://www.steelcase.com/content/uploads/sites/2/2022/08/2022_SC_GlobalReport_EMEA-DE.pdf.

compared to only about one third of managers (Fig. 9.3). Since this traditionally hierarchical character still characterises many office environments in companies, many employees prefer to work from home, even if it is only from the sofa. Because at home they can organise their work better and have more privacy. In contrast, many managers globally prefer to work in the office because they experience sufficient privacy there due to the private offices available to them.[7]

Based on these findings, I have created a figure (Fig. 9.3) that visualises these points in order to really see the differences mentioned above.

These are again very exciting figures for us, as it shows that the people who have more opportunities to retreat also come to the office more. So far so good! But the question was only inadequately asked. After all, it is also about finding out why employees come to the office. That is actually the key that must be turned first.

Because many come to the office precisely to meet people, to collaborate, to hold meetings or for social interaction. Even those who come to work quietly can be provided with retreat spaces through sensible planning. It is important to find out what people need to work well and efficiently. And then transform this knowledge into spatial structures. Very often I see that people do it the other way round and somehow derive their needs from the spatial structures. But that drives our efficiency in the wrong direction and our satisfaction with the office down.

In order to build meaningful working environments, we have to engage with people and ask critical questions.

9.3.3 Private Areas Are Also Very Important in the Office

Change in the way and place of work is profound and is expected to continue, especially as companies search for the optimal form of hybrid working. In the current era of constant change, companies are striving to develop strategies to manage their existing offices. One often hears

---

[7] Steelcase Inc. Das neue Zeitalter der hybriden Arbeit. Was die Angestellten jetzt brauchen – Wie Gemeinschaft am Arbeitsplatz entsteht (Global Report). February, 2022. Available at: https://www.steelcase.com/content/uploads/sites/2/2022/08/2022_SC_GlobalReport_EMEA-DE.pdf.

64 %	Areas for hybrid collaboration	62 %	Niches for single use in hybrid meetings
57 %	Reservable workspaces	61 %	Privacy
52 %	Informal areas for exchange with colleagues	58 %	Fully or partially enclosed work areas
49 %	Large number of rooms designed for collaboration	52 %	Flexible furnishing
47 %	Sustainable office furniture		

Fig. 9.4 What people value in the office based on Steelcase's findings mentioned in the text (Gauer Consulting)

discussions about making work environments purely collaborative and social. There is even talk of turning the office into a sort of social clubhouse.

While it is undoubtedly of great importance to design the workplace in a way that helps to foster a strong corporate culture and create a sense of belonging, the office needs to offer even more (Fig. 9.4). In today's world, people spend more time in video conferences than ever before. Providing the appropriate technical platforms is only part of the solution. People also need spaces that meet the demands of new ways of working.

Figure 9.4 illustrates Steelcase's findings on what people value in the office, and thus shows which aspects need to be taken into account when designing offices to meet the needs of employees.[8]

In order not to exceed the scope, I would like to focus in the following on three of the points shown in Fig. 9.4.

Firstly, the results show that 64 per cent of people highly value hybrid collaboration areas in the office,[9] which I personally find extraordinarily high. I think we need to think much more about—and here is where I come back to strategy and analysis—why people want to come to the

---

[8] Steelcase Inc. Das neue Zeitalter der hybriden Arbeit. Was die Angestellten jetzt brauchen – Wie Gemeinschaft am Arbeitsplatz entsteht (Global Report). February, 2022. Available at: https://www.steelcase.com/content/uploads/sites/2/2022/08/2022_SC_GlobalReport_EMEA-DE.pdf.

[9] Steelcase Inc. Das neue Zeitalter der hybriden Arbeit. Was die Angestellten jetzt brauchen – Wie Gemeinschaft am Arbeitsplatz entsteht (Global Report). February, 2022. Available at: https://www.steelcase.com/content/uploads/sites/2/2022/08/2022_SC_GlobalReport_EMEA-DE.pdf.

office. Does it really make sense to create so many hybrid opportunities if everyone ends up sitting alone in a cubicle making video calls? I do not think so. It would also be a sustainable possibility to consider when which team members come into the office so that they can work together. Creating zones that allow space for project work or collaborative get-togethers.

Another element is the bookable workstations. To be frank, I think they are highly overrated and see them more as part of an emotional strategy for stability because employees are afraid of not getting a (good) spot. Which, by the way, I completely understand. But when I then ask my clients about their experiences with bookable workplaces, I usually get the feedback that they have either been abolished after a short time or are not used. Instead, we should ask ourselves how workplaces can be designed so that employees feel comfortable in them and the fear of not having a good workplace is taken away from them in the run-up to the workplace change.

This builds a bridge to the topic of privacy, which is always and rightly considered extremely important in the new world of work. I am actively working with my research partners on the question: How much privacy do people need to be able to work healthily and efficiently? With the widespread open space approaches, we often work against human needs. It is important that we allow a critical discourse here again in order to create a sustainable working environment.

9.4 What Does this Mean for Leadership?

9.4.1 For Managers

This is where leadership plays a very active role and where you, as a manager, can show whether you have really internalised this new way and new world of working. It is very much about leading by example and embracing the new office and working world. In my experience, however, this only works if you yourself have dealt with the issue openly and honestly yourself.

Very often I experience managers telling me that everything is clear and that they know what it is all about. It is no big deal. But in reality, it is a big deal, and many workplace change initiatives fail not because of the action plan, but because of active, honest and authentic implementation.

Because what we forget in today's fast-paced and hectic times is our authenticity. I have mentioned this in previous chapters, but I want to mention it again because it is truly the be-all and end-all of success. No matter what I am thinking or feeling, I am constantly sending out these signals. We psychologists speak of the so-called "honest signals" of communication. As the Austrian philosopher Paul Watzlawik so aptly said: "One cannot *not* communicate".[10]

Our language is only about 50,000 years old, a small and modest part of the world's history of communication. We can lie with language, but not with our human signals (body language, tone of voice, facial expressions, gestures).

If our environment—in this case our employees—does not take us seriously because they do not believe what we say, then we have lost before we have started. Because a working environment is only successful if people are allowed to actively shape it and actively live and experience it together. Even the best office design cannot change this.

9.4.2 For Employees

For employees, it is crucial that their superiors understand this new working world, actively live it and try it out. But that they also allow their employees to try it out.

Again, an honest and open approach to the new world of work is needed. Because it is much more complex than merely new layouts with new furniture. It is a new mindset that must and should be allowed to emerge. But this will not happen at the push of a button, it will take hard work.

---

[10] Watzlawick, P., Beavin, J. H., & Jackson, D. D. Pragmatics of Human Communication. New York W. W. Norton, 1967:51.

10

Emotional Leadership as a Booster for New Work Environments

The emotionally intelligent leader should be able to recognise how employees relate to their environment and understand how they feel. Given that, according to many philosophers who study emotions, (a) a particular emotion arises as a result of our own evaluative process and (b) emotions can have their own drive and motivation,[1] an emotionally intelligent leader can more accurately assess a person's behaviour based on their emotional disposition and values.

On the other hand, as our goals and values change, so do our emotions as signals of what we consider important or useful. Accordingly, the meaning people attach to their environment and the objects in it changes, as do their future goals.[2]

So, our environment reflects what we consider important, and we interact with it accordingly. For example, a socially anxious person places a high value on meeting performance targets. Because the company culture rewards efficiency and creativity, the person is more likely to interact with other employees to ensure productivity and new ideas, despite their

---

[1] Cain, T. Emotion and Value. Philosophy Compass. 2014;9(19):702–712.
[2] Peterson, J. Maps of Meaning: The Architecture of Belief. New York: Taylor & Frances/Routledge; 1999.

aversion to social interactions. This process is smoother for the person if they are supported, and their potential is nurtured.[3]

10.1 What Employees Want

Employees want enough space at work to realise their potential. When both organisational and personal values are aligned, affective commitment to the organisation is more likely.[4] Employees' affective commitment increases when they are treated with respect and a future-oriented mindset, when a superior supports them personally and helps them realise their potential. This benefits both the employee and the organisation. A competent manager will identify where a person's development is hindered and help them to develop their skills and abilities.

When preparing employees for the transition to a more functional and dynamic multi-space office environment, the following skills should be fostered to maintain competence and reduce the perception of environmental stressors: Self-management, self-awareness, interpersonal skills, resilience and courage, empathy and emotional intelligence, critical thinking and questioning of one's own beliefs, goal setting and implementation, attention and focus, attentive listening and a positive attitude towards work, the world and people.

10.2 How Much Can a Leader Give?

Leaders and managers in the New Work environment must increasingly take on the role of development partners and performance helpers, using as many situations as possible to actively promote the development of

---

[3] Dionne S., Yammarino, F., Atwater, L. Transformational leadership and team performance. 2004;17(2):177–193.

[4] Finegan, J. The impact of person and organizational values on organizational commitment. Journal of Occupational and Organizational Psychology. 2000;73(2):149–169.

their employees.[5] The demands and expectations of employees and society are high.

Currently, the trend in managing modern employees is strongly in the direction of excessive support. As mentioned above, the list of skills that a manager should foster in employees is long and complex. The mindset of the modern employee has changed very much into a consuming and demanding one. People feel the need to be valued. Employees want to be perceived by the employer as the person they are. During the covid pandemic, this need has become even more pronounced. The number of people working from home has increased dramatically. Many people appreciate this opportunity. Yet, many also feel disconnected from the rest of the organisation, and under-appreciated.

10.2.1 Too Few Workers for Future Economic Performance

The situation has changed in favour of the employees. Employees are reorienting themselves because they can. They realise that they are in demand. In the past, after an interview, it was said: We'll get in touch with you and let you know what happens next. Today the applicant says: I will think about whether I want to work for your company.

In a study published in 2015, the Basel-based research institute Prognos shows: For the year 2040, a skilled labour gap of 3.9 million workers is expected in Germany. Despite previous efforts to secure skilled labour, the deficit will continue to rise. This clearly shows the need for action with regard to the design of framework conditions for better utilisation of labour market potentials.[6]

---

[5] Hackl, B., Wagner, M., Attmer, L., Baumann, D. New Work: Auf dem Weg zur neuen Arbeitswelt. 1st ed. Wiesbaden: Springer; 2017. DOI: 10.1007/978-3-658-16266-5.

[6] Ehrentraut, O. (Prognos AG). Arbeitslandschaft 2040. München: Vereinigung der Bayerischen Wirtschaft e. V. 2015. Available at: https://www.prognos.com/sites/default/files/2021-01/20150521_prognos_arbeitslandschaft2040-final.pdf.

10.2.2 Problem Factor Quiet Quitting

Quiet quitting is not, by definition, the old form of internal resignation, i.e. working just enough to avoid being fired and leaving as soon as something new comes along.

Quiet quitting means doing only what you are obliged to do. If people are told "Please finish the presentation for the client meeting by 6 pm". Then people are gone at 6:01 pm. They are doing their job well and delivering good results, but they are not doing more than what is in the contract. When the employer asks them to do more and stay longer, they often react with incomprehension, because that is not what they agreed to in the contract. Many are then unwilling to go the extra mile. This generation simply calculates: How much will you give me, then I will give you the corresponding performance.

Meanwhile, companies are being put through their paces by employees. The advantages and disadvantages are analysed in detail, and it is examined exactly how much freedom, incentives, flexibility, working models, etc. a company offers.

This is a completely different way of thinking that has developed and that companies cannot always keep up with. There is also the critical question of whether this can foster and produce healthy and sustainable personal and economic growth in the long run. Selfishness is important and helps us move forward, but at the end of the day there needs to be a positive outcome for both sides.

10.3 How Much Responsibility Does a Manager Have to Take on?

I think we need to be a bit careful about the amount of room for action and responsibility that we give to leaders.

Ethical dilemmas may well arise in the development of meaning and values, i.e. the promotion of certain assumptions and beliefs may interfere with the development of genuine well-being or the building of a healthy personal identity. However, an organisation that wants to promote affective commitment, workplace loyalty, vitality and, at the same time, considerateness in multi-space offices should aim for values that reach employees on a deep and existential level.

Emotionally intelligent leaders demonstrate a deeper understanding of their employees and teams, which supports the use of the transformative skills they can apply to their people. They also help to foster team cohesion, communication and teamwork.

10.4 New Working Environments: An Emotional Process

10.4.1 Transformation Is a Challenge

The transformation of the world of work is a challenge for the development of trust between employees and in their relationships with each other and, in particular with managers.

Especially within teams, a quarter of all employees seem to have a lower level of trust in their colleagues, and this number increases the more employees work from home.[7]

The Corona pandemic and the new world of work and realities that are now being developed very actively and rapidly, with their hybrid, mobile, more open concepts, thus seem to be putting increasing strain on social ties and trust in relationships within organisations. Change is happening fast and on several levels at the same time.

On the one hand, we work differently, and on the other, when we are actually in the office, we increasingly have different office structures (multi-space office), which in themselves are an opportunity and an enrichment, but from a human and emotional point of view also require a period of adjustment and adaptation. However, we try to do everything at the same time and this brings us to our human limits.

---

[7] Koneberg, F., Lehr, J., Seyda, S. & Werner, D. Herausforderungen und Chancen hybrider Arbeit (Kompetenzzentrum Fachkräftesicherung (KOFA), Eds.). June, 2022. Available at: https://www.kofa.de/daten-und-fakten/studien/herausforderungen-und-chancen-hybrider-arbeit/.

All the more reason for companies to invest systematically in the development of optimal working environments. This involves promoting hybrid and mobile working in a meaningful and sustainable way, while actively supporting the new working environments with their office concepts (multi-space or activity-based working) and developing them efficiently, in a way that creates value and is inclusive.

This includes, in particular, creating office environments that encourage employees to meet and interact socially. As a manager, you are particularly called upon here to ensure the fragile structure is held together.

Modern working environments harbour a lot of emotion with substantial explosive power. It is about us, as people, as managers and as employees, learning to treat each other in a new way and reorienting ourselves in a world that is more open and flexible, but at the same time more sensitive and fragile.

10.4.2 Leadership Is the Balance Between Desires and Possibilities

Managers are trying to do the right thing. They offer their employees a collection of benefits—from salary increases, bonuses and other incentives—and move towards hybrid working models to offer more flexibility and individuality. However, this can make the relationship with employees feel very business-like and not offer them what they actually want and need: Appreciation and a sense of belonging to the company.

The physical office can play an important and influential role here. The office with its working environment can communicate values and help create a community in the workplace that provides a sense of belonging. The workspace takes on the role of the company's body language, thereby communicating the prevailing culture and showing what the management cares about.

The office is hugely important to employees. Especially these physical places where work is done can be used by companies as a strategic resource.

Offering more remote working and salary increases is one step, but it is not enough to bring about sustainable systemic change. This is because even monetary incentives only have a short-term motivating effect. The habituation effect occurs very quickly and then the salary increase is completely normal and no longer inspires.

It is the task of employees and managers to create the right atmosphere in the workplace and make the company more resilient, so that it can successfully survive in uncertain times when framework conditions are constantly changing.

Further Reading

Achoba, M. I., Majid, R. A., & Obiefuna, C. O. (2021). The relationship between workplace window and seating arrangement. *In IOP Conference Series: Materials Science and Engineering, 1051*(1), 012103.
Ashino, B. (2020). https://commons.wikimedia.org/wiki/File:UZABASEOffice_2.jpg
Asutay, E., & Västfjäll, D. (2012). The perception of loudness Is influenced by emotion. *PLoS ONE, 7*(6), e38660. https://doi.org/10.1371/journal.pone.0038660
Bakker, A., & Demerouti, E. (2007). The job demands-resources model: State of the art. *Zeitschrift für Managerpsychologie, 22*(3), 309–328.
Becker, C., Kratzer, N., & Lanfer, S. (2019). Neue Arbeitswelten: Wahrnehmung und Wirkung von Open-Space-Büros. *Arbeit, 28*(3), 263–284. https://doi.org/10.1515/arbeit-2019-0017
Bernstein, E., & Waber, B. (2021, September 2). The truth about open offices. Harvard Business Review. https://hbr.org/2019/11/the-truth-about-open-offices
Block, J., Boeing, N., Briegleb, T., Dettling, D., Gatterer, H., Horx, M. (2022). (Eds.), Horx, T., Kibala, J., Pfuderer, N., Reichel, A., Schuldt, C., Tewes, S., Wolf, M. Zukunftsreport 2023.

Further Reading

Bull, M., & Brown, T. (2012). Change communication: The impact on satisfaction with alternative workplace strategies. *Facilities, 30*(3–4), 135–151. https://doi.org/10.1108/02632771211202842

Cain, T. (2014). Emotion and value. *Philosophy Compass, 9*(19), 702–712.

Carsten, S., Gisinger, E., Kibala, J., Kirig, A., Muntschick, V., Papasabbas, L., Pfuderer, N., Pfuderer, N., Seidel, A., & Schuldt, C. (2021). *Zukunftstinstitut. Neue Arbeit.*

Cavanaugh, M., Boswell, W., Roehling, M., & Boudreau, J. (2000). An empirical examination of self-reported work stress among US. managers. *Zeitschrift für angewandte Psychologie, 85*(1), 65–74. https://doi.org/10.1037/0021-9010.85.1.65

Chang, C., & Chen, P. (2005). Human response to window views and indoor plants in the workplace. *HortScience, 40*(5), 1354–1359.

Chen, C., & Huang, J. (2007). How organizational climate and structure affect knowledge management - The social interaction perspective. *Internationale Zeitschrift für Informationsmanagement, 27*(2), 104–118. https://doi.org/10.1016/j.ijinfomgt.2006.11.001

Colenberg, S., Jylhä, T., & Arkesteijn, M. (2021). The relationship between interior office space and employee health and well-being–a literature review. *Building Research & Information, 49*(3), 352–366.

Coradi, A. (2018). Mentale Gesundheit als Erfolgsfaktor. In *Zukunft der Arbeit - Perspektive Mensch. 2. Aufl* (pp. 357–367). Springer Gabler. https://doi.org/10.1007/978-3-658-22099-0_27

Crummenerl, C., Paolini, S., Perronet, C., Lamothe, I., Ravindranath, S., Schastok, I., Buvat, J., Manchanda, N., Aggarwal, G., & Chakraborty, A. (2020). The future of work: from remote to hybrid. Capgemini Research Institute. Luettavissa. Luettu, 2, 2020. https://www.capgemini.com/fi-en/wp-content/uploads/sites/27/2020/12/Report-The-Future-of-Work.pdf

DAK. Psychreport. (2023). Entwicklungen der psychischen Erkrankungen im Job: 2012–2022. 2023. https://caas.content.dak.de/caas/v1/media/32628/data/3983614e98a936fe7d7dd70f3dac2e73/dak-psychreport-ergebnispraesentation.pdf

Dionne, S., Yammarino, F., Atwater, L., & Spangler, W. (2004). Transformational leadership and team performance. *Journal of Organizational Change Management, 17*(2), 177–193. https://doi.org/10.1108/09534810410530601

Ehrentraut, O. (2015). (Prognos AG). Arbeitslandschaft 2040. München: Vereinigung der Bayerischen Wirtschaft e. V. https://www.prognos.com/sites/default/files/2021-01/20150521_prognos_arbeitslandschaft2040-final.pdf

Entringer, T. (2022). *Epidemiologie von Einsamkeit in Deutschland*. Institut für Sozialarbeit und Sozialpädagogik eV Kompetenznetz Einsamkeit.

Ergan, S., Radwan, A., Zou, Z., Tseng, H. A., & Han, X. (2019). Quantifying human experience in architectural spaces with integrated virtual reality and body sensor networks. *Journal of Computing in Civil Engineering, 33*(2), 04018062.

Espe, H., & Schulz, W. (1983). Room evaluation, moods, and personality. *Perceptual and Motor Skills, 57*(1), 215–221.

Evangelischer Fachverband für Arbeit und soziale Integration (EFAS) (Ed.). Handout Grundlagen Konfliktbearbeitung & Konfliktmanagement. https://www.efas-web.de/files/teges/Teges_Handout_Konflikt_FINAL_SCREEN.pdf

Finegan, J. (2000). The impact of person and organizational values on organizational commitment. *Journal of Occupational and Organizational Psychology, 73*(2), 149–169.

Flade, A. (2020). *Kompendium der Architekturpsychologie: Zur Gestaltung gebauter Umwelten*. Springer Fachmedien Wiesbaden GmbH.

Franken, S. (2016). *Führen in der Arbeitswelt der Zukunft. 1. Aufl.* Springer Gabler. https://doi.org/10.1007/978-3-658-11613-2

Galliker, S., Igic, I., Elfering, A., Simmer, K., & Job-Stress-Index, N. (2022). Monitoring von Kennzahlen zum Stress bei Erwerbstätigen in der Schweiz. (Gesundheitsförderung Schweiz, Ed.).

Gerdenitsch, C., Korunka, C., & Herte, G. (2017). Need-supply fit in an activity-based flexible office: Eine Längsschnittstudie während eines Umzugs. *Environment and Behavior, 50*(3), 273–297. https://doi.org/10.1177/0013916517697766

Gimpel, H., Lanzl, J., Regal, C., Urbach, N., Wischniewski, S., Tegtmeier, P., Kreilos, M., Kühlmann, T., Becker, J., Eimecke, J., & Derra, N. D. (2019). *Gesund digital arbeiten?! Eine Studie zu digitalem Stress in Deutschland.* Projektgruppe Wirtschaftsinformatik des Fraunhofer FIT. https://doi.org/10.24406/fit-n-562039

Haans, A., Kaiser, F. G., & de Kort, Y. A. (2007). Privacy needs in office environments: Development of two behavior-based scales. *European Psychologist, 12*(2), 93–102.

Hackl, B., Wagner, M., Attmer, L., & Baumann, D. (2017). *New Work: Auf dem Weg zur neuen Arbeitswelt. 1. Auflage.* Springer Gabler. https://doi.org/10.1007/978-3-658-16266-5

Haner, U., & Wackernagel, S. (2018). Kurzbericht zur Studie Wirksame Büro- und Arbeitswelten. Ausgewählte Erfolgsfaktoren für eine wirksame Gestaltung von Büro- und Arbeitswelten. http://publica.fraunhofer.de/dokumente/N-494183.html

Haner, Udo-Ernst, & Wackernagel, S. (2020). Kurzbericht zur Studie «Wirksame Büro- und Arbeitswelten». Ausgewählte Erfolgsfaktoren für eine wirksame Gestaltung von Büro- und Arbeitswelten. http://publica.fraunhofer.de/dokumente/N-494183.html

Hassan, A. (2007). Human resource development and organizational values. *Journal of European Industrial Training, 31*(6), 435–448.

Hawkley, L. C., & Cacioppo, J. T. (2010). Loneliness matters: A theoretical and empirical review of consequences and mechanisms. *Annals of Behavioral Medicine, 40*(2), 218–227.

Inrix. (2023, March 14). Inrix 2022. Global Traffic Scorecard. INRIX Global Traffic Rankings. Available at: Inrix. https://inrix.com/scorecard/#city-ranking-list

Jiranek, H., & Edmüller, A. (2015). *Konfliktmanagement – Konflikte vorbeugen, sie erkennen und lösen.* Freiburg/München.

Jungsoo, K., & de Dear, R. (2013). Workplace satisfaction: The privacy-communication trade-off in open-plan offices. *Journal of Environmental Psychology, 36*, 18–26. https://doi.org/10.1016/j.jenvp.2013.06.007

Jurecic, M. (2020). Gut zu wissen: die Wirkung von Büroumgebungen auf unterschiedliche Arbeitstypen. In S. Wörwag & A. Cloots (Eds.), *Zukunft der Arbeit – Perspektive Mensch* (pp. 331–340). Springer Gabler.

Knight, C., Olaru, D., Lee, J., & Parker, S. (2022). The loneliness of the hybrid worker. MIT Sloan Management Review.

Koneberg, F., Lehr, J., Seyda, S., & Werner, D. (2022, June). Herausforderungen und Chancen hybrider Arbeit (Kompetenzzentrum Fachkräftesicherung (KOFA), Ed.). https://www.kofa.de/daten-und-fakten/studien/herausforderungen-und-chancen-hybrider-arbeit/

Koordinationsgruppe für die Statistik der Unfallversicherung UVG (KSUV) c/o SUVA. (2022). Unfallstatistik UVG 2022.

Kozusznik, M., Peiro, J., Soriano, A., & Escudero, M. (2018). Out of sight, out of mind? The role of physical stressors, cognitive appraisal, and positive emotions in employees' health. *Environment and Behavior, 50*(1), 86–115. https://doi.org/10.1177/0013916517691323

Kunze, F., & Zimmermann, S. (2022). Die Transformation zu einer hybriden Arbeitswelt: Ergebnisbericht zur Konstanzer Homeoffice Studie 2020–2022. http://nbn-resolving.de/urn:nbn:de:bsz:352-2-ai5pzcioansj3

Lai, L., Chau, K., Davies, S., & Kwan, L. (2021). Open space office: A review of the literature and Hong Kong case studies. *Work, 28*(3), 749–758. https://doi.org/10.3233/WOR-203408

Lamothe, I., Duruflé, B. T., & Kirstein-Bandmierowski, M. (2021, September 3). Trust at the heart of hybrid working. Capgemini. https://www.capgemini.com/insights/expert-perspectives/trust-at-the-heart-of-hybrid-working/

Lanfer, S., Becker, C., & Göritz, A. (2019). Well-being in open space offices: Die Rolle von Büromerkmalen und psychosozialen Arbeitsbedingungen. *Work, 68*, 317–332. https://doi.org/10.3233/WOR-203378

Lazarus, R., & Folkman, S. (1984). *Stress, Appraisal und Coping.* Springer Publishing Company.

Lévi-Strauss, C. (1967). *Strukturale Anthropologie.* Suhrkamp.

M.O.O.CON. (2012). Activity Based Working denkt Bürokonzepte weiter. https://docplayer.org/16326549-Activity-based-working-denkt-buerokonzepte-weiter.html

Maidani, E. A. (1991). Comparative study of Herzberg's two-factor theory of job satisfaction among public and private sectors. *Public Personnel Management, 20*(4), 441–448.

Mainka-Riedel, M. (2013). *Stressmanagement – Stabil trotz Gegenwind. 1. Auflage* (pp. 5–43). Springer Gabler. https://doi.org/10.1007/978-3-658-00931-1

Maslow, A. H., & Mintz, N. L. (1956). Effects of esthetic surroundings: I. Initial effects of three esthetic conditions upon perceiving "Energy" and "Well-Being" in faces. *The Journal of Psychology., 41*(2), 247–254. https://doi.org/10.1080/00223980.1956.9713000

Mayer, J. D., Salovey, P., & Caruso, D. R. (2004). Emotional intelligence: Theory, findings and implications. *Psychological Inquiry., 15*(3), 197–215.

Metaj, R. (2019). Architekturpsychologie, Einfluss auf die Arbeit im Büro, Lehrbuchverlag.

Microsoft Corporation. (2021). The next great disruption is hybrid work: are we ready?. https://www.microsoft.com/en-us/worklab/work-trend-index/hybrid-work

Morrison, R., & Smollan, R. (2019). Open plan office space? If you're going to do it, do it right: A fourteen-month T longitudinal case study. *Applied Ergonomics, 82.* https://doi.org/10.1016/j.apergo.2019.102933

Oommen, V., Knowles, M., & Zhao, I. (2008). Should health service managers embrace open plan work environments? A review. *Asia Pacific Journal of Health Management, 3*(2), 37–43. https://www.researchgate.net/

publication/27475865_Should_Health_Service_Managers_Embrace_Open_Plan_Work_Environments_A_Review

Pelz, W. (2016). Transformationale Führung–Forschungsstand und Umsetzung in der Praxis. Wirksame und nachhaltige Führungsansätze: System, Beziehung, Haltung und Individualität, 93–112.

Pelz, W. Transformationale Führung: Vorteile und Wirkung (neue Studie). https://www.transformationale-fuehrung.com/index.html

Peterson, J. (1999). *Maps of meaning: The architecture of belief.* Taylor & Frances/Routledge.

Robinson, B. (2020). What studies reveal about social distancing and remote working during coronavirus. https://www.forbes.com/sites/bryanrobinson/2020/04/04/what-7-studies-show-about-social-distancing-and-remote-working-during-covid-19/#562a9a7b757e

Sadri, G. (2012). Emotionale Intelligenz und Führungsentwicklung. *Public Personnel Management, 41*(3), 535–548. https://doi.org/10.1177/009102601204100308

Sanchez, J. A., Ikaga, T., & Sanchez, S. V. (2018). Quantitative improvement in workplace performance through biophilic design: A pilot experiment case study. *Energy and Buildings, 177*, 316–328.

Schaufeli, W., & Taris, T. (2014). A critical review of the job demands-resources model: Implikationen für die Verbesserung von Arbeit und Gesundheit. In G. Bauer & O. Hämmig (Eds.), *Bridging occupational, organizational and public health* (1st ed., pp. 43–68). Springer. https://doi.org/10.1007/978-94-007-5640-3

Schaufeli, W. B., & Bakker, A. B. (2004). Job demands, job resources, and their relationships with burnout and engagement: A multi-sample study. *Journal of Organizational Behavior., 25*(3), 293–315. https://doi.org/10.1002/job.248

Scrima, F., Mura, A., Nonnis, M., & Fornara, F. (2021). The relationship between workplace attachment style, design satisfaction, privacy and exhaustion in office employees: A moderated mediation model. *Zeitschrift für Umweltpsychologie, 78*(4), 101693.

Starker, V., Roos, K., Bracht, E. M., & Graudenz, D. (2022). Kosten von Arbeitsunterbrechungen für deutsche Unternehmen. Auswirkungen von Fragmentierung auf Produktivität und Stressentwicklung.

Steelcase Inc. (2021). Changing expectations and the future of work – Insights from the pandemic to create a better work experience. https://www.steelcase.com/content/uploads/2021/02/2021_AM_SC_Global-Report_Changing-Expectations-and-the-Future-of-Work-2.pdf

Steelcase Inc. (2022, February). *Das neue Zeitalter der hybriden Arbeit. Was die Angestellten jetzt brauchen – Wie Gemeinschaft am Arbeitsplatz entsteht* (Global Report). https://www.steelcase.com/content/uploads/sites/2/2022/08/2022_SC_GlobalReport_EMEA-DE.pdf

Tarafdar, M., Maier, C., Laumer, S., & Weitzel, T. (2020). Explaining the link between technostress and technology addiction for social networking sites: A study of distraction as a coping behavior. *Information Systems Journal, 30*(1), 96–124.

Ward, A. F., Duke, K., Gneezy, A., & Bos, M. W. (2017). Brain drain: The mere presence of one's own smartphone reduces available cognitive capacity. *Journal of the Association for Consumer Research, 2*(2), 140–154. https://doi.org/10.1086/691462

Watzlawick, P., Beavin, J. H., & Jackson, D. D. (1967). *Pragmatics of human communication.* W. W. Norton.

Watzlawick, P., Beavin, J. H., & Jackson, D. D. (1969). *Menschliche Kommunikation* (Vol. 2, p. 24). Huber.

Williams, S. (2002). Strategic planning and organizational values: links to alignment. *Human Resource Development International, 5*(2), 217–233. https://doi.org/10.1080/13678860110057638

Wörwag, S., & Cloots, A. (2020). *Zukunft der Arbeit – Perspektive Mensch.* Springer Fachmedien.

Yang, L., Holtz, D., Jaffe, S., et al. (2022). The effects of remote work on collaboration among information workers. *Nature Human Behaviour, 6*, 43–54. https://doi.org/10.1038/s41562-021-01196-4

Zheng, W., Yang, B., & McLean, G. (2010). Linking organizational culture, structure, strategy, and organizational effectiveness: Die vermittelnde Rolle des Wissensmanagements. *Journal of Business Research, 63*(7), 763–771. https://doi.org/10.1016/j.jbusres.2009.06.005

GPSR Compliance

The European Union's (EU) General Product Safety Regulation (GPSR) is a set of rules that requires consumer products to be safe and our obligations to ensure this.

If you have any concerns about our products, you can contact us on

ProductSafety@springernature.com

In case Publisher is established outside the EU, the EU authorized representative is:

Springer Nature Customer Service Center GmbH
Europaplatz 3
69115 Heidelberg, Germany